ALASKA'S SAVAGE RIVER

Inside Denali National Park and Preserve

To one of my favorite people — Dianne Walker

VALERIE WINANS

Valerie Winans

PO Box 221974 Anchorage, Alaska 99522-1974
books@publicationconsultants.com—www.publicationconsultants.com

ISBN: 978-1-59433-454-2

eBook ISBN: 978-1-59433-455-9

Library of Congress Catalog Card Number: 2014934068

Manufactured in the United States of America.

Contents

Introduction

WHEN OUR DAUGHTER AND SON-IN-LAW FIRST SUGGESTED
we apply for a job as campground hosts in Denali Park
and Preserve, our reaction was no; we could not possibly
do such a thing. Dan and Natalie had stayed in the park
while vacationing in Alaska and heard there would be an
opening for campground hosts the following season. In
spite of our rejection, they returned home with information
on how to apply for the job. We then thought, why not?
"Let's apply and just see what happens," said my
husband. Dave had talked about going to Alaska for
years. By serving as half of a campground-host team,
I could help make Dave's dream come true.

We were hired! Our assignment was at Savage River
Campground, which meant we would spend four and a
half months at a rustic campground with our only connection to the outside world being a park radio to dispatch—or we could drive 12.8 miles to Riley Creek.

We packed the trailer with everything we thought we
would need and, along with our dog, Remington Beagle,

we were soon on our way to Alaska. Just getting to our destination was an adventure. The drive through Canada and along the Alaska Highway provided scenery that adjectives do not suffice in describing. We also loved seeing the wildlife and stopping at unique places with interesting histories. To say that we enlarged our horizons is an understatement. The experience changed our lives.

We were provided with orientation and training, but learned more about campground hosting by working with experienced hosts. Carol and Larry Hensel not only gave us on-the-job training, they also became lifelong friends.

As part of the process of adjusting to this new environment, I asked a lot of questions and read everything I could get my hands on about the area. The more I learned, the more information I sought; and thus this book.

My purpose is to give readers not only a picture of present days in Savage River Campground, but a picture of the past in order to connect the people of the past with the people of the present so they may better appreciate this unique area and its stories.

Oh, I can't tell you at what point the dream ceased being just Dave's and became mine also, but one season was not enough—and we found ourselves returning for a second!

One

First Days at Savage River

THE GATE WAS CLOSED AND PADLOCKED. THE LANE ON the other side of the gate still had patches of snow—even though it was mid-May. This is where Dave and I would live for the next four months. We wanted a better look.

Leaving our dog, Remington Beagle, in the truck, we walked through snow and around the gate into Savage River Campground. Soon we came to a bend in the road that obliterated our view of the park road and the truck. We were alone in the park, and I was anxious. Then we noticed some tracks in the snow, and animal feces in the road—and we knew we were not alone. My anxiety increased and I felt the need to make noise to give notice to any nearby animal that humans had entered their habitat. Dave, on the other hand, wanted quiet. He wanted to see a big grizzly bear, or a wolf, or a moose—something on this walk in the park. I only wanted to see those animals from inside the safety of the truck.

The first signs of civilization we found were two buildings, one on each side of the road. The one on the left was an "SST," which stands for "sweet-smelling toilet." It was, in fact, a pit toilet. Although it didn't smell as bad as some pit toilets, I would not say it was sweet-smelling. The building on the right was a restroom with running cold water and flush toilets. It was built in 1955 to serve the new campground. Beyond those buildings, we saw a sign that read Campground Host Site. There it was: home, at last. Still covered in snow.

"Okay, I'm good. Let's go back to the truck."

"No, I want to snoop around some more. We should go down this road and see what is at the end," said Dave. Only with persistent urging did he consent to returning to the truck and safety.

If a small hike scared me, how was I going to live here for the next four months? I wondered. A couple days later, we moved into our campsite in the wild, away from the main camp at Riley Creek. There was no running water yet at Savage River and everything was still frozen. We would have to get by with the water we had in the tank of our trailer and bottled water. The gate was open, guests were on their way to the park, and we needed to be ready for business.

Dave was antsy to explore more of the park before people arrived; so off we went. This time, I was prepared for the hike with warm clothes, wool socks, gloves, and a camera around my neck. I was not yet brave enough to head out over the tundra, so we stuck to the road system in the park. We didn't get far before we came to a bend with two trails heading off in opposite directions. We took the fork to the far left. I stepped on every stick and talked loudly to my husband, hoping once again to ward off danger. Dave shushed me and walked a bit ahead. As he

VOLUNTEER CAMPGROUND HOST

On our first visit to Savage River Campground we found our campsite covered in snow.

Savage River as it was when we arrived at the park in 2008 complete with grizzly bear in the distance.

turned a bend in the road, he stopped, motioned with his arm for me to come along; then he put his index finger to his lips, signaling me to be quiet. He urged me forward. Probably a rabbit or a caribou, I thought. Yikes! It was three grizzly bears! They were about fifty feet ahead, and one looked right at us. I froze momentarily—until my extensive campground-host training clicked in. I slowly backed up. I kept walking backward until I could no longer see the bears, while at the same time reminding myself to breathe. I now had an approximate sixty-foot head start, but bears can run very fast. The problem was that once my feet started to move fast they would not slow down again. It was the old fight-or-flight response, and flight was the only option. Having been warned not to run from bears, I justified running faster than I had since I was in grade school because the bears could not see me. Was I sure? I slowed down long enough to look back. No bears. No Dave. Where in the hell is Dave?! The trailer was in sight—thank you, God. I was going to make it. Where was Dave? When I reached the end of the campsite, only feet from the door and safety, I saw Dave strolling up the lane. Are you kidding me?! Well, you are on your own buddy, I thought. I stepped inside the trailer, where I felt much safer and where I could finally breathe again at a normal rhythm. After what seemed like an eternity, Dave came inside. The first thing he said is, "Did you get a picture?"

"Did I get a picture? Are you crazy? I was happy to get away from there with my life!"

"You're making a mountain out of a mole hill. Those bears had no interest in us at all. It was a big mother with two cubs. The cubs were last year's cubs, I'm sure."

It's going to be one long, scary summer, I thought. How in the world can I be a campground host if I don't get out and about and know what's going on in the park? But it will be easier to be outside once there are other people around. I assured myself. There was safety in numbers.

Days went by without seeing any bears. We saw snowshoe hares every day, and lots of birds, but few bears and no wolves. Most of the time, the campground was full; so there were people to talk with, problems to solve, and work to do. I was more confident each day that I would be able to do this job. Dave, on the other hand, needed no confidence building. He was the quintessential Boy Scout and loved every minute. He was in his element. His experience and his love of the outdoors made him the perfect campground host.

I finally built up enough courage to walk the whole campground by myself or with Remington Beagle. I even went down to the bluff overlooking the river at the edge of the campground. As I walked the lonely lane to the end of the bluff my senses were on alert. My eyes searched for signs of danger, and my ears strained to hear every sound. Seeing the valley unfold its mysteries helped me suppress my fear of danger. From the bluff, the view was breathtaking. Everything was bigger here, with mountains all around. The valley was so large that we could see for miles. Soon, I could identify some of the mountains. To the south

The song of the White-crowned Sparrow can often be heard in Savage River Campground.

was Fang, and to the north was Mt. Margaret. The spot at the end of the bluff called to me, tugged at me, talked to me. Each time I returned to the siren's call it looked different. One day, there was Mt. McKinley in all of its splendor; the next day, fog so thick I couldn't even see Fang. One day, I saw McKinley sharp and clear against a bright blue sky. Across the river from the bluff was a small herd of caribou, and the white-crowned sparrow provided a symphony for my pleasure. I was no longer afraid.

"THERE I SAT ON A DOWNED TREE, WATCHING, LISTENING, ABSORBING THE SOUNDS, SIGHTS, AND FEELINGS OF THE LAND. I WAS CONTENT AND FULFILLED, ONE WITH THE LAND. I DIDN'T FEEL AS IF I OWNED IT – I WAS, SIMPLY, A PART OF IT, AND IT WAS BEAUTIFUL AND WONDERFUL."

Sidney Huntington

Two

Savage Campground

WITHIN A NATIONAL PARK LARGER THAN SOME countries there is much to see and do. The confluence of Jenny Creek and Savage River is a very special place in an abundance of special places – it is magical. People are attracted to this place as if pulled by primordial forces. Hundreds of years ago, the people of the interior undoubtedly traveled through, hunted, fished, and camped here—as they do today. It is the first site where visitors camped and viewed "the mountain."

The bluff that overlooks the river at the end of the Savage River Campground provides a view of the mountain called Fang where the glacier feeding the river originates. About a mile and a half downstream is the terminus of the glacier. The Savage River Bridge is there, and from that spot, and from almost anywhere on the Savage Loop Trail, a visitor can get a panoramic view of the Savage River valley. It's hard to imagine a glacier filling up that valley! As the glacier melted, the size and force of the river must have been savage indeed. In the spring, the river is fast-moving and filled with silt from the glacier, but in the fall it gets shallower and clearer. However, the river doesn't get its name from its nature – it gets it from a man.

This brave man came to Alaska in search of gold. Thomas Strand was a Snohomish Indian from the state of Washington. He worked in the mines for various miners who had filed claims, and that is when he began to be called Tom Savage. Although it would be an insult in our culture today, it was not given much importance in those days. He even filed some gold claims under the name Tom Savage; so he must not have minded the name too much. After he stopped working in the mines, Tom hunted and trapped the Savage Fork area – to the extent that people started calling the river Savage's River. Tom eventually married and raised a family near the community of Ferry, Alaska. Tom's grave is in a family cemetery near Ferry; a tribute to the man who left his mark and his nickname for posterity.[2]

Savage River Campground is the second camp you will encounter as you travel along the park road. It is 12.8 miles from the main road. It is rustic. There is no electricity, although water is accessible from pumps placed throughout the park. There are two bathrooms with running cold water and flush toilets, and two pit toilets. If you can move beyond the luxury of a hot shower and full hookups, there are wonders to behold and lessons to be learned. The campsites are in a pocket of spruce trees situated near the tree line. As you near mile 12.8 on the park road, the river valley opens up for a view that will astound. The hard, rocky ground takes you to the river, but if you leave the taiga and venture across the tundra you will soon learn what muskeg is.

View of the Savage River Valley. Fang Mountain, where Savage River originates, is in the distance.

Our vocabulary and geographical knowledge increased each day as Dave and I explored our new habitat. Taiga is a Russian word meaning evergreen forest. Black spruce, with its straight, tall, skinny trunks and spindly, short branches are common on the taiga. There is also aspen, birch, and poplar in the boreal forest found below the tree line. Tundra comes from the Finnish word tunturi which means treeless. Various kinds of plant life grow on the tundra, depending on available moisture. Although Savage River Campground is located in an area with conifers and some willow, you don't have to walk far to be on the tundra. Walking on the tundra is arduous due to sporadic areas of muskeg—a bog of partially decayed vegetable matter. The area appears to be a flat or rolling plain, but when you take a step, your foot might go into the muskeg up to your knee. You can't travel very far on this sponge like bed before exhaustion sets in.

This photo from the Candy Waugaman collection shows the original Savage Camp with Mt. McKinley in the background.

Savage River Camp   Mt. McKinley National Park   Mt. McKinley in distance

Season's Greetings

Mt. McKinley Tourist & Transportation Co

Remnants of the original Savage Campground.

One of the co-hosts at Savage River Campground invited me to hike with her one day. We waded across Savage River at a narrow point and traversed up a small hill. We decided to hike to the next ridge. The landscape is so expansive it was difficult for us to discern distance. Walking though the muskeg was a chore, one step was on ground as hard as rock and the next we would be up to our knees in muskeg. It took us longer than expected to reach the top of the ridge, and by the time we got there we were not inclined to return the same way. Walking along the ridge, we found what looked like an easy trail back to the road. It was an easy trail most of the way down the

The sign at the entrance to
Savage River Campground
and Remington Beagle.

Savage Loop Trail and Savage River
with the park road in the distance -2009.

hill—but when we reached the bottom we found a creek in the brush that was swiftly moving and too wide to jump across. We followed the creek back in the direction of Savage River Campground. We found fresh bear scat, which made us nervous. We also found a huge moose antler that had been shed. It was amazingly heavy. Moose must be exhausted hauling two of those around all day. Eventually, we came to a place where we could easily cross the stream, and we were soon back at the campground. It felt as though we had walked many miles, but when I checked my pedometer we had traveled less than two miles.

There is a trail near Savage River Campground that leads to Savage Cabin. This cabin originated with the park road and is used by rangers during the winter as a refuge when they patrol the park. Interpretive programs for visitors and some of the bus tours also stop at Savage Cabin. I enjoyed walking with Remington Beagle up the park road past this trail. Since dogs are not allowed on trails, R. Beagle did not see the cabin or the doghouses used for sled dogs. About a mile beyond Savage Cabin is the Savage River Bridge. This marks the spot on the road that is the start of the Savage River Loop Trail, and the end of the road for private vehicles during most of the year.

Savage River Loop Trail takes you close to the river for about a mile, where you cross a wooden bridge and return to the park road on the other side of the river. Although the trail is uneven and rocky, it is an easy hike—unless you choose to leave the trail. If you are bold enough, you can leave the trail at the bridge and continue to hike along the river or you can go to the top of Mt. Margaret and on from there. The view improves with the elevation, and offers spectacular views of the valley. We routinely saw ground squirrels, marmots, and ptarmigan along this trail, and many people see Dall sheep here. There are places near the park road for picnicking, and there are also some pit toilets for your convenience.

Many folks who passed by Savage River have embraced its offerings. The spot where Jenny Creek flows into the Savage River was recognized early on as a perfect place to make a camp for travelers. The river provided much in terms of a water source, a place to fish, a draw for animals that could be viewed by visitors, and water rushing over rocks also provides a lullaby for sleeping. Travelers always want to see Mt. McKinley and this spot is also the first opportunity as a person travels into the park from the railroad to view the mountain. Where taiga and tundra meet there are trees to provide shade and firewood, as well as wide open spaces for a spectacular view.

The original camp is long gone but another campground lies adjacent to that spot. Cursory exploration uncovers part of an old water system and boards used at the original Savage Camp. You can close your eyes and imagine yourself back in time, residing in a tent camp set up along Jenny Creek. There is a horse corral, a cook's tent, and a social hall. If the mountain is "out," you can get a clear view of it. There's a phonograph playing in the social hall, and the folks who work here are busy fixing meals, cleaning, and organizing activities. If you try, you can almost hear the whinny of a horse, pots banging in the cook's tent, and the laughter of happy people.

Three

Denali: The Town and the National Park

THE TOWN IS CALLED "THE CANYON" AND IS A SEASONAL place that opens for tourists in May and closes in September. It is the gateway to Denali National Park and Preserve. It is located on the George Parks Highway, between Anchorage in the south and Fairbanks in the north. The Alaska Railroad cut the first path through this canyon, marking the way before the seasonal community or any road ever existed.

The community perches on the edge of a canyon carved out of rock by the Nenana River. The canyon is deep and its walls are steep. The water moves through the narrow spots rapidly, making whitewater visible everywhere on the river as it passes by Denali the town. If you take a switchback road up a mountain on the edge of town you will be rewarded with an awesome view of the town, the river, one of its bridges, and its valley.

In the summer months, the town's population consists of visitors and those who serve them. Many employers provide housing for their workers as nearly all of the employees come from all over the United States as well

A view of the canyon town called Denali Park from near the top of Mt. Healy in 2009.

as other nations. Most visitors drive north to the park from Anchorage, where they have just deplaned or come ashore from a cruise ship. Some arrive via the Alaska Railroad, some in rented vehicles, and some hearty individuals drive their own vehicles from destinations around the world.

The town offers beautiful hotels, great restaurants, and specialty shops. Uniquely Alaskan items are available from local artisans, such as carvings, jewelry made from local gems, furs, birch bowls, and much more. Activities include rafting the Nenana River, helicopter rides, fixed-wing flights over Mt. McKinley or landing on a glacier, four-wheeler tours, golfing, and dinner theatre.

Leaving the George Parks Highway to enter the park, the first place you see is Riley Creek Campground. It is the largest campground in the park and the nearest to all services. It is within walking distance of the canyon town of Denali Park and its amenities. If you want a different experience, all of the campgrounds in the park provide a starting point for hiking, wildlife encounters, scenic views, and meeting people from all over the world.

My favorite trail at Riley Creek Campground takes hikers to the base of the railroad bridge, which is where some of the first settlers lived. If you look carefully, you will see remnants of their life along the creek.

Near the Visitor Center at Riley Creek Campground is a trail that leads to the top of Mt. Healy. It is a somewhat strenuous hike, but doable even for the occasional hiker. I would have made it to the top, with bragging rights to the summit of Mt. Healy, but for a grizzly bear that took up residence that day along the trail. People who had reached the summit could not descend due to the bear, and those wanting to reach the top chose to leave rather than have a confrontation with such a formidable foe.

If the town is the gateway to the park, the park road is its passport to adventure. In her thesis, "From Myth to Reality," Gail Evans describes the road as the place where nature and culture meet.

> "IN THE PARK'S EARLY HISTORY, CONSTRUCTION OF A WINDING, NINETY-MILE ROAD IN A REMOTE, HARSH, UNFORGIVING NATURAL ENVIRONMENT, DOMINATED ALL OTHER ADMINISTRATIVE EFFORTS. THIS HERCULEAN EFFORT TO CREATE CULTURAL ACCESS TO ABUNDANT WILD NATURE IN MOUNT MCKINLEY NATIONAL PARK EXEMPLIFIES THE TRANSFORMATION OF THE PHILOSOPHY OF DEMOCRATIC USE BY "ALL THE PEOPLE" INTO REALITY."

This narrow winding road was constructed between 1922 and 1937. During the fifteen years of construction, the Alaska Road Commission worked in partnership with the National Park Service to accomplish this awesome "linear cultural artifact."[1] Some improvements have been made since that time by widening the road, moving some sections of the road to higher ground, as well as grading and maintenance. It was recognized at the outset that a road into the park would be needed if the public was going to be able to access the wilderness. Several suggestions were made for routes into the park. In 1917, USGS geologist Stephen Capps stated that there should be a road "reaching from the railroad westward to McKinley. Such a route... has already been provided by nature. A remarkable series of low passes...form a natural highway through this rugged area. For centuries the game herds have used these passes, and deeply worn trails (that) lead from valley to valley along the easiest route."

Eventually the road would reach ninety miles into the park and afford panoramic views of Mt. McKinley. In addition, it offered a way back to the railroad and civilization for the miners and homesteaders living far out in the bush. Visitors have always been driven as far as the road would allow, first in touring cars and later in buses. The road opens a window to the wilderness for many who otherwise would not be able to partake of its beauty.

Railroad connection to the park and improvements made to the road contributed to increased tourism. The seasonal town was established in those early years, and as the "linear cultural artifact" progressed farther into the park, each year it extended the passport for visitors to go from town to park and experience more and more of the awesome natural phenomenon now known simply as Denali.

At the beginning of the season, just prior to the arrival of the first buses in the park, the road is opened to private vehicle traffic as far as Teklanika. What a great opportunity it is to take this road trip, stopping along the way wherever you wish and for as long as you wish. The first view of Mt. McKinley is where the park road first approaches Savage River. Closer and more breathtaking views of the mountain are possible from other spots farther along the park road past Teklanika—but that first view of the mountain from Savage is special. With or without a view of the mountain at Savage River, the landscape is spectacular. The rivers are braided here because silt from the glaciers that feed the rivers eventually block the routes of a stream causing it to find an area of less resistance and thus the water heads off in another direction. The road from Savage River Campground to Teklanika goes up and down in and above the tree line. The boreal forest is pristine and the views from higher elevations display the green growth of spring, as well as various-colored minerals in the rocks of the mountains. The landscape also offers views of the beautiful rolling piedmont, with occasional patches of birch, alder, spruce, and willow.

As you travel into the park you might notice huge boulders in the middle of nowhere. They are called erratics. One of Webster's definitions for erratic is "transported from an original resting place especially by a glacier." Sure enough, these magnificent rocks, some as big as a two-story house, have been deposited by glaciers.

The higher elevations are home to Dall sheep. At the start of the season, you will often see the ewes with their lambs. The bears, not long out of hibernation, are busy eating their favorite spring meal of roots and squirrels. If they can find them, they dine on baby caribou and moose as well. Caribou have been on the move to find summer

Moose are often seen in the park. More people are injured by moose than by bears in the park as people don't view them as the danger they actually are.

Mt. McKinley showing both the north and south peaks, and the park road snaking off on the right. Visitors to the park place a view of this mountain on the top of their list of things they most want to experience.

Yellow Tailed Warbler – a frequent visitor in Savage River Campground.

The Ptarmigan camouflage by going from brown in the summer to white in the winter. They abound in Denali Park and Preserve and feed on willow buds, seeds, leaves, and berries. There is a myth that the town of Chicken, Alaska got its name because the founding members wanted to call the town ptarmigan, but as no one could spell ptarmigan they just named it Chicken.

Caribou are called reindeer when they are domesticated. They migrate through the park eating the grasses and plants found on the tundra.

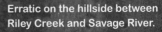

Erratic on the hillside between Riley Creek and Savage River.

Magpies compete with Ravens to see who can make the most noise.

grazing for some time, but occasional herds are still seen in the valleys. Moose are everywhere, from the visitor center parking lot to the farthest reaches of the park. The grizzly bears, caribou, and moose are a sight, but the birds are just as pleasing.

The ptarmigan change color, from pure white in the winter to multiple brown shades in the summer. This early in the season, they are mostly part white with the brown of their summer adornment beginning to show. The grey jays, ravens, and magpies make their presence known through their raucous calls and high-jinks. The white-crowned sparrows and the yellow-rumped warblers contribute with sweet sounds for balance.

Four

Early People of the Park

As we oriented ourselves to our new environment, we wanted to learn more about this amazing place. We purchased and read books, and we used park resources to learn more. As people of the present we needed more information about the people of the past. As we talked to visitors we recognized that they also had a hunger for more information about this special place and its' past.

In researching the history of the park we learned about the people who after visiting here wanted to protect it and preserve it for others.

The national park in Alaska which congress created last spring is one of the monster spectacles of the world. To say that it rises 20,300 feet above sea level and that it is the loftiest peak in America is to convey no idea whatever of its grandeur. There are several mountains in the Himalayas which materially exceed its height, one which rises more than 25,000 feet above sea level; and yet Mount McKinley, to the

OBSERVER IS LOFTIER THAN ANY OF THESE. THE REASON IS
THAT THE GREATEST HIMALAYAS ARE SEEN FROM VALLEYS
SEVEN TO TEN THOUSAND FEET IN ALTITUDE, WHILE MOUNT
MCKINLEY RISES ABRUPTLY FROM VALLEYS THREE THOUSAND
FEET AND EVEN LESS IN ALTITUDE.

Fairbanks Daily News-Miner,
"The Monster of Mountains," *July 11, 1917*

In 1906, as Charles Sheldon stood on the ridge of a
mountain looking at a trail that followed the contour of
the land, he did not know that the trail would eventually
turn into a 90 mile long road connecting the mining community of Kantishna with the railroad at Riley Creek. This
mountainous area was beautiful and wild, and Sheldon
fell in love with it. During that summer, fall, and winter
of 1906 he lived in the area near the Toklat River and Mt.
McKinley to observe the seasonal habits of large game
animals.[1] He specifically wanted to study Dall sheep because
there wasn't much known at that time about the Ovis dalli.[2]

As Sheldon and his packer, Harry Karstens, tramped
along looking for sheep, they made their camp on the
piedmont and enjoyed looking at the Alaska Range in the
distance. Harry Karstens proved to be a capable packer,
and their friendship which developed during this time
lasted a lifetime. While they were camped Sheldon saw
"ground squirrels, marmots that whistled on the moraine,
Canada jays flew about, the tree sparrows and intermediate
sparrows sang continually, and wax-wings and northern
shrikes were particularly plentiful. White-tailed ptarmigan
with broods of chicks were near; the wing-beats of ravens
passing overhead hissed through the air; Arctic terns flew

gracefully over the meadows; and golden eagles soared above the ridges. Old bear diggings were everywhere, but no large animal was seen except a big bull caribou."[3] Amazingly enough, the 21st century camper can have the same experience due to the preservation of this area as a refuge, and it was Charles Sheldon who was instrumental in getting legislation passed to make the area a national park and preserve.

After Charles Sheldon's first visit to Alaska in 1906, he was committed to the establishment of a national park and wildlife preserve near Mt. McKinley. He was convinced that when the railroad passed near, the Dall sheep would be obliterated because their meat was a prime commodity for railroad crews and roadhouses. He had many friends in sportsman's clubs and in politics, and he used his influence to promote a wildlife preserve. With the help of others, his dream became a reality in 1917 when it was signed into law by President Wilson.[4] Sheldon wanted the park to be called Denali, and stated in his book, *The Wilderness of Denali*.

> "THE INDIANS WHO HAVE LIVED FOR COUNTLESS GENERATIONS IN THE PRESENCE OF THESE COLOSSAL MOUNTAINS HAVE GIVEN THEM NAMES THAT ARE BOTH EUPHONIOUS AND APPROPRIATE. IN A COMPARATIVELY SHORT TIME THE INDIANS WILL BECOME EXTINCT. CAN IT BE DENIED THAT THE NAMES THEY GAVE TO THE MOST IMPOSING FEATURES OF THEIR COUNTRY SHOULD BE PRESERVED? CAN IT BE TOO LATE TO MAKE AN EXCEPTION TO CURRENT GEOGRAPHIC RULES AND RESTORE THESE BEAUTIFUL NAMES— NAMES SO EXPRESSIVE OF THE MOUNTAINS THEMSELVES, AND SO SYMBOLIC OF THE INDIANS WHO BESTOWED THEM?"[5]

In spite of Sheldon's plea, Congress called the park Mt. McKinley National Park. Finally, in 1980, under the Alaska National Interest Lands Conservation Act, the park's name was changed to Denali Park and Preserve, but the name of the mountain remains McKinley.

One hundred years ago, the land looked pretty much as it does now except for the few contributions made by man since the area became a national park in 1917. The park road is the most significant manmade mark as it snakes ninety miles inward. It can be spotted from thousands of feet in the air as it follows the natural contours of the land, taking a route through the mountains used by people and animals for hundreds of years before anyone thought of building a road from the trail.

At the end of the road is Kantishna, a gold-mining community; although before the gold miners traveled this path, explorers, mountaineers, and scientists led the way. In the late eighteenth century, George Vancouver and Ferdinand von Wrangell were among the first explorers to note the "distant and stupendous mountains covered with snow."[6] When William Seward purchased Alaska from the Russians in 1867, the highest point on the North American continent had not been recognized as such. It wasn't until 1897 when William Dickey surveyed the mountain, declared it to be over 20,000 feet in height, and gave the mountain the name it has today: Mount McKinley. He named the mountain for the man "who had been nominated for the presidency."[7] Although the mountain had several different Indian names, Denali is the original Athabascan name and some still prefer to call it Denali, which means "the great one."

Mt. McKinley 20,322 feet high – the highest peak on the North American continent.

Dall sheep are named after William H. Dall. They were over hunted because their meat was a much desired commodity. Charles Sheldon fought for the establishment of a preserve for these animals which eventually resulted in Denali Park and Preserve.

A National Park is Born

HARRY P. KARSTENS RECENTLY APPOINTED BY SECRETARY
FALL TO BE SUPERINTENDENT OF MT. MCKINLEY NATIONAL
PARK, ARRIVED IN FAIRBANKS ON THE NENANA TRAIN LAST
EVENING AND IS KEPT BUSY TODAY IN RECEIVING THE
CONGRATULATIONS OF HIS MANY FRIENDS.

Fairbanks Daily News-Miner,
"Harry Karstens is On the Job," *June 11, 1921*

Mt. McKinley National Park was in its nascent stage a park
and preserve in name only as there were no funds to hire
anyone to protect its resources. Every year Congress was
lobbied for funds for the newly established park, but other
priorities always topped the list. Finally, in 1921, funds
were allocated to the park.[8] During all the years Sheldon
and others fought for funds, he was also currying favor for
his choice of lead ranger (superintendent) of the park. The
person he believed to be the best candidate for the job was
his friend Harry Karstens.

When he was only 19 years old Harry Karstens came to
the Klondike like many others because he was lured by the
promise of gold. He found himself in a place called
Seventymile, south of Eagle, Alaska. He became proficient
at dog mushing and trailblazing and worked delivering mail
on a primitive trail between Eagle and Valdez. He later
moved on to Fairbanks, and began delivering mail to
Kantishna. His knowledge of this area made him a perfect
candidate to be Charles Sheldon's packer. Sheldon
convinced that he was just the man to take the leadership
role in the new park and preserve because of his experience

with Karstens on the piedmont. Karstens did have the skills and ingenuity necessary to build a park infrastructure using only the resources found on the land. When he arrived to begin his work as superintendent, the park had not even been surveyed. He brought with him Woodbury Abby who did the first survey of the park's boundaries.[2] Karstens hiked the park behind Abby's survey team because he didn't have a horse. He was

Dan Kennedy, the first concessionaire in Mt. McKinley National Park.

Photo courtesy of Candy Waugaman collection.

very concerned about poaching, but first he had to have a park headquarters and a place to live. Working alone, he cleared a spot near Riley and Hines Creeks, where he erected the first building in the park, from logs he cleared himself.

Harry Karstens was concerned about protecting the wildlife in the park; he knew that once the railroad was completed there would be more visitors. Aware that part of his job was to make the park accessible to people, he hired a concessionaire to provide destinations and diversions for visitors. Although Karstens had several interested parties for the job of park concessionaire, a former horse packer and guide from Nenana, Dan Kennedy, was chosen as the first concessionaire in Mt. McKinley National Park.[10]

Dan Kennedy had a big job to do. While he was busy setting up a tent camp at the confluence of Jenny Creek and Savage Fork, he also worked on the road leading from the train station to the camp, which was nothing more than a brushed-out trail. By July 4, 1923, the road was not even "cruised out"[11] all the way to Savage Camp, and groups of important guests were due to visit the park on July 7, 8, and 15. Although Kennedy prioritized working on the road over completing the necessary facilities at the camp, he did have a crude camp established by July 7 at Jenny Creek and Savage River. Karstens was not happy with the lack of progress on the camp because he planned to take his guests out there. However, the first visitors, including a congressional party, a group from the Brooklyn Eagle newspaper, and President Harding's party, did not have time for the twelve-mile ride to Savage River.[12] (The railroad car used by President Harding during this trip can be viewed at Pioneer Park in Fairbanks.)

Nineteen twenty-four did not bring Karstens any more satisfaction with the concessionaire. Savage Camp was not fully operational until June of that year, and the other two camps contracted for were not in operation at all. Savage Camp consisted of only eight small brown-canvas tents, and a cook tent/dining room. There were only sixty-two visitors that year, which was a losing proposition for both parties. Kennedy established his company under the name Mt. McKinley Tourist and Transportation Company and had the mayor of Fairbanks, Alaska, Thomas Marquam, as an advisor. They were looking for additional ways to bring in money and began to arrange guided hunting trips out of Cantwell. This

James Galen, when he served as president of Mt. McKinley
Tourist and Transportation Company, had a favorite white horse
named Rabs. After his sudden passing, the horse was sold to a
former employee as Galen said he wished the horse would go to
a good home when it was no longer useful.

Photo courtesy of the Candy Waugaman collection.

**Savage Camp when it was operated by the
Mt. McKinley Tourist and Transportation Co.**

*Courtesy of National Park Service, Denali National Park
and Preserve Museum Collections DENA 21947.*

was a cause for more friction between Kennedy and Karstens because the area used for hunting was along the border of the park, and there was no easy way to patrol that area. Relations between Karstens and Kennedy did not improve; and as a result, Kennedy sold his company in June 1925.[13]

With James Galen as president, Thomas Marquam as vice-president, and Robert E. (Bobby) Sheldon as the on-site manager of the Mt. McKinley Tourist and Transportation Company, the operation began to run smoothly. The company worked in partnership with the National Park Service, the Alaska Railroad, and the Alaska Road Commission to provide services in the park for the next seventeen years. The company decided that "its main camp would remain at Savage Camp, regardless of how far road construction progressed; it did so because of the camp's nearness to the railroad, the spectacular Mt. McKinley view, and the plethora of nearby points of interest."[14]

THE ENDEAVOR OF THE BUREAU OF BIOLOGICAL SURVEY TO BUILD UP THE MARKET QUALITY OF THE ALASKAN REINDEER IS TAKING ACTIVE FORM. O.J. MURIE, FIELD REPRESENTATIVE OF THE BIOLOGICAL SURVEY, LEFT FOR MCKINLEY PARK STATION YESTERDAY, TAKING WITH HIM A PARTY OF EXPERIENCED CATTLEMEN AND WOODSMEN WHO WILL ATTEMPT THIS FALL TO CORRAL A NUMBER OF BULL CARIBOU FOR BREEDING PURPOSES.

THE SCENE OF OPERATIONS WILL BE THE HEAD OF SAVAGE FORK, IN THE PASS BETWEEN THE SAVAGE AND THE SANCTUARY, WHERE THEY WILL COMMENCE IMMEDIATELY TO

CONSTRUCT A CATCHING PEN. THE MAIN CORRAL WILL
ENCLOSE AN AREA OF AN ACRE OR MORE… MR. MURIE HAS
STUDIED THIS COUNTRY CLOSELY, AND BELIEVES THAT IT IS
THE MOST FAVORABLE LOCATION FOR THE EXPERIMENT… IT
MAY BE POSSIBLE BY THIS METHOD OF CROSSING TO DEVELOP
AN ANIMAL OF GREATER WEIGHT AND BETTER MEAT QUALITY
THAN EITHER THE REINDEER OR CARIBOU, AS HAS BEEN THE
CASE WITH BEEF CATTLE.

Fairbanks Daily News-Miner,
"Murie Securing Caribou Bulls," *August 12, 1922*

The Mt. McKinley Tourist and Transportation Company, in an effort to provide more opportunities for tourists, worked with the Alaska Road Commission to establish a road "for nine miles up the west side of Savage River valley to a tent complex dubbed Caribou Camp."[15] This was near the camp that Olaus Murie erected for his caribou studies in 1922.) The company took tourists up this road in stage-coaches, and later by automobile. "The trip was called "the Big Game Drive,"[16] along which could be seen sheep, caribou, bears, and foxes.

Extended trips into the park consisted of a "two-day saddle-horse trip…to the head of Savage River, then back to camp via Sanctuary River; another trip headed to Igloo Creek; while the most expensive trip, played out over eight days, took visitors all the way to Copper Mountain (now Mt. Eielson). In order to support those trips, by 1928, the concessionaire had built tent camps at Igloo Creek, Toklat River, and Copper Mountain. The company also erected a tent at Polychrome Pass, presumably as a mid-day rest stop."[17]

R. E. SHELDON, MANAGER OF THE MCKINLEY TOURIST AND TRANSPORTATION COMPANY, RETURNED LAST NIGHT FROM A TRIP MADE TO THE COMPANY'S SAVAGE RIVER CAMP. HE STATES THAT A MESS HOUSE WILL BE COMPLETED WITHIN THE NEXT FEW DAYS. A DINING TENT WITH BOARD FLOORS AND SIDEWALLS AND A COMMUNITY TENT WITH DANCE FLOOR, EACH 24 X 40 FEET ARE BEING BUILT AT THE PRESENT TIME AND WILL BE IN READINESS FOR THE TOURIST SEASON. THE DINING ROOM WILL ACCOMMODATE 60 PEOPLE AT A SITTING, AND THERE WILL BE SLEEPING ACCOMMODATIONS FOR A MAXIMUM OF 75. A NEW ORTHOPHONIC VICTROLA WILL PROVIDE MUSIC FOR DANCING. MR. SHELDON SAYS THAT THE COST OF THE CAMP WILL RUN WELL OVER $10,000.

Fairbanks Daily News-Miner, **"Sheldon Completes Trip Savage Camp,"** *May 26, 1926*

The Mt. McKinley Tourist and Transportation Company continued to improve services, and the number of tourists increased each year. Bobby Sheldon and his crew loved what they were doing at Savage Camp, and their good will was felt by the visitors. The trip to the park was a long and difficult one at that time – there was no road from the lower 48, and the crew at Savage did their best to make the trip worthwhile for their customers. But at the same time, a hotel was being built at McKinley Park Station. When the hotel was completed, Savage Camp was moved to Mile 66 in the park. The company's contract to run the concession was not renewed because the U.S. government decided to run the concession, and then legislation was passed giving the concession to the Alaska Railroad as it was also operating the new hotel.

Washington - President Roosevelt signed the bill authorizing the Alaska Railroad to take over the transportation and tourist accommodation facilities in Mt. McKinley National Park which authorized a $30,000 appropriation for use of the Railroad for this purpose.

Fairbanks Daily News-Miner, **"Railroad To Run Park Facilities,"** *March 30, 1940*

The Mt. McKinley Tourist and Transportation Company continued to operate the camps through a temporary contract until the end of the 1941 season. Tourist travel to Alaska came to a halt on December 7, 1941, and continued throughout World War II. During the war, the U.S. military, in cooperation with Canada, built the highway known as the Alcan. The highway starts at Dawson Creek, British Columbia, Canada, and ends at Delta Junction, Alaska, where it joins the Richardson Highway and continues on to Fairbanks, Alaska. Although there were challenges traveling the new highway, for the first time the lower forty-eight were connected with Alaska by road. Traveling the Alcan (now called the Alaska Highway) was its own adventure, but despite the difficulties of the journey to the last frontier, the road had a huge effect on tourism post World War II.

Five

Some Days in the Campground

THERE WAS A KNOCK ON OUR TRAILER DOOR. "JUST WANTED to let you know there are some bears down by the river."

"Grab the camera and get the telephoto lens," said Dave.

"Yeah, well, I sure hope we will need a telephoto lens!" I said.

Grabbing the camera, the telephoto lens, and the bear spray, I charged out of the door with my arms full. "I don't believe I'm doing this."

When we reached the bluff, I was relieved to see that the bears were the required three football fields away. (There were no down markers or anything, I was just estimating the distance.) Soon there were twenty or more people watching the sow and her two cubs dig for the roots of a plant called the Eskimo Potato.

Dave decided he needed to get closer for a better picture—I reminded him that was totally against the rules. He said he would follow the rules, but just get a little bit closer. This made me very anxious, but off he went. The other people soon filtered back to the campground. I thought, if they waited for a bit they would be able to get pictures of the bears eating a man and his camera. Fortunately that did not happen (it was a really nice camera) and Dave did take some good pictures.

―――・―――

We learned that two young women were missing. They were employed in the canyon town of Denali Park and did not report for work. They were dropped off in the Savage River area, either at the bridge or at the campground, and then spent the night at Savage River Campground with some friends before they left on foot the next morning. The girls have been missing for several days and officials are concerned for their welfare. We have seen helicopters and fixed-wing planes every day searching the area. There are also groups searching for them on foot that organized their search at Savage Campground. Soon their parents have arrived from the lower forty-eight. Finally, one of the parents received a cell phone call from her daughter; the women are in an area called Dry Creek. This is the first place where they could obtain a signal enabling her to call for help. The young ladies are located and picked up. They are surprisingly well, and don't seem to have suffered much from lack of food and exposure to the elements.

Later, we learned that the girls were not lost in Savage River Canyon—they were in Fairbanks. They made up the story about being lost. Of course we were relieved that they were alright while at the same time outraged at the waste of time and money.

―――・―――

Dave was doing a morning walk-about, making a list of dead trees that needed to be removed for safety reasons. Stopping to look at a tree, he heard a huffing noise behind him—and turned to face two grizzly bears only twenty feet away. Dave raised his clipboard and shouted, "Get out! Get out of here, bears!" They did not move. They stood there, sizing him up. (So much for the theory that the human voice will repel bears because they are not used to hearing it.) At that moment, a park service employee drove into the park in his Jeep, which encouraged the bears to move on. They walked past Dave into the campground. Dave asked the guy in the Jeep to go to the end of the campground and alert a group of scouts there that bears are in the park. Then Dave shouted to warn the other campers. When Dave returned to our host site, the bears were coming right down the road behind our trailer. The bears snooped around for a bit and then walked on down to the river. They stayed in the park just long enough to get everyone's adrenaline pumping.

At the host-site campfire and storytelling night, a camper told of his bus ride into the park. At Teklanika they see a mother moose and her baby being chased by a bear. The mother moose ran into a stream with her calf trying to avoid the bear. Then, along came another mother moose and baby being chased by a different bear. The first bear stopped and joined the second bear and together they were successful in having baby moose for lunch. It seems brutal, and although I would prefer not to witness such a scene, I can appreciate it is just the circle of life.

One day, Dave and I encountered our friend Russ, the photographer. He told us there was a baby moose across the river that had been abandoned by its mother. The mother moose had come to the river with her twins but crossed the river with only one calf because one refused to cross. The mother finally left it on the bank and continued on her way. She had not been seen since.

Later, as we stood on the banks of the river watching the baby moose, we meet a bus driver who has been watching it for a while. He said the bleats of the calf were getting weaker. I took some pictures of the baby moose before we continued down the trail. Our goal was to see some Dall sheep in the heights; but no luck. We were, however, rewarded with the sound of water tumbling over rock and the melodies of various birds as we enjoyed the amazing view.

When we return to the parking lot, we saw that the baby moose had made its way to the river for a drink. Dave and I took more pictures and video of him. There were also several photographers lined up with their tripods and cameras, all set to photograph the calf and his fate. Since it was highly likely that he would come to a bad end, and I did not want to witness whatever happened, we left. About a half mile down the road, we saw buses stopped in the road—and a bear. The bear was headed toward the bridge. It is park policy that nothing be done to interfere with the wildlife, so nothing could be done to intervene for the baby moose. Filled with anxiety for the calf, we return to our camp. The next day we learned that no one at the bridge ever saw the bear, and no one knows what happened to the baby moose. It was just gone. Maybe the mother came back for it, or maybe it wandered off. I hope he is well.

We were sitting by our campfire when we heard, "Bear! It's a bear!" Dave hurried to the road to see a lady standing on a rock on the opposite side of the road. "I was walking down the road when I heard a sound behind me and there was a bear," she said. "I was so startled that I jumped up on this rock. The bear looked right at me, but just kept on walking down the road."

I have a picture in my mind of the bear sauntering down the road chuckling to himself about scaring that lady—and how silly she was to jump up on that little rock.

———

Bus driver to another bus driver: "See anything interesting today?"

"No, only some stone sheep."

"Were they moving very much?"

"Not since the Ice Age."

When searching mountain tops for white Dall sheep, it is easy to mistake white rocks for sheep. Although there is such a thing as Stone sheep, they are not found in Denali Park. Bus drivers tell their riders if they see wildlife to shout out and they will stop the bus. I'm sure after a number of stops for white rocks it gets tiresome.

———

I was by the road in front of our trailer talking to some people in a motorhome when a pickup truck pulled up behind them. The people in the truck were straining to look around the motorhome so I thought they were just anxious to get by. When the motorhome left, the truck pulled up to where I was standing. I recognized them as the campers in the site next to ours. "There's a bear on our campsite!"

"Great! We charge extra for sites with bears."

"No, really! We were sitting at our picnic table, and a bear walked right up to us. We jumped in our pickup and left."

Soon after we heard from campers on the next loop that a bear walked through their campsite and into the

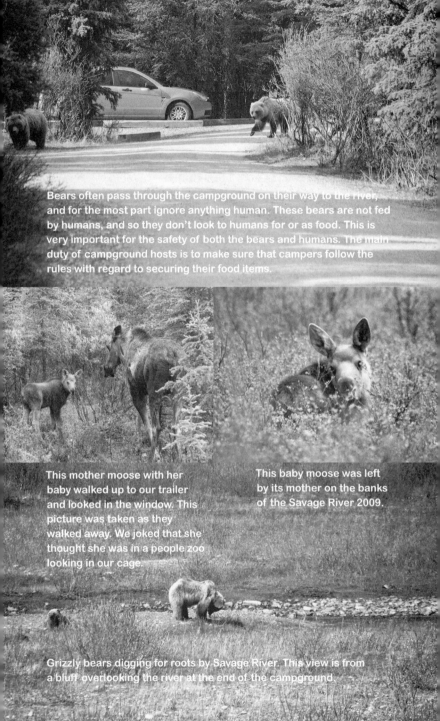

Bears often pass through the campground on their way to the river, and for the most part ignore anything human. These bears are not fed by humans, and so they don't look to humans for or as food. This is very important for the safety of both the bears and humans. The main duty of campground hosts is to make sure that campers follow the rules with regard to securing their food items.

This mother moose with her baby walked up to our trailer and looked in the window. This picture was taken as they walked away. We joked that she thought she was in a people zoo looking in our cage.

This baby moose was left by its mother on the banks of the Savage River 2009.

Grizzly bears digging for roots by Savage River. This view is from a bluff overlooking the river at the end of the campground.

woods. Chalk up another one for a grizzly bear that gets kicks out of scaring the crap out of people and then chuckling under his breath about funny humans.

———

"Oh, look Dave. There's a moose and her baby right next to our trailer. She is looking in our window as though she is visiting a human zoo. How funny."

———

I woke up one morning to find that our vistas had collapsed; I could only see as far as the tallest trees around Savage River Campground. The monotone gray of the sky had eased its way down the sides of the mountains and covered everything with a white/gray ethereal blanket. When I took a closer look, I realized it was raining pretty hard – and I had rounds to do.

After waiting for a while to see if the rain would let up, I decided I must prepare and head out—rain or no. First I put on long underwear and wool socks. Next came blue jeans, a turtleneck, rain pants, and my heavy campground-host jacket. A rain hat and stretch gloves completed the ensemble. I grabbed a plastic grocery sack for expired permits and a clear plastic bag to cover the clipboard. I was ready to go.

Once outside, the rain was not so bad. I was dry under all my gear, and it was strangely pleasant. A rainy day meant a quiet campground. The campers would stay inside their campers or leave the park for other adventures.

———

We saw bear prints going up the outside wall of one of the bathrooms. It looked as though the bear "walked" up the wall with his front paws and looked in the window. This was no cub as the window was quite high on the wall. I guess we had a Peeping Tom in the park.

———————

Depending on which way the wind blows, from time to time a smoky haze covers everything in Denali Park. The haze is from wild fires that are eighty miles or more away. The bulletin board in the EDR (employee's dining room) reports that there are two substantial fires. The closest one is at Bear Creek, about eighty miles from us. The Bear Creek fire has burned more than 15,847 acres. The other fire is at Zitziana, which is about fifty miles southeast of Tanana. It has burned 8,800 acres. The policy is not to fight the fires unless buildings are in danger. Some days have been so smoky that we can hardly see the mountains. The smoke causes the sun to appear red in the sky; the sunsets are eerily pretty.

———————

Burls are a popular décor item found in Alaska. It is believed that burls form on trees due to acidity in the ground from naturally occurring arsenic in the soil. This causes cell blockage and new cells grow around the cells that are blocked. Those new cells become blocked, new cells grow around those, etc. Dave found a burl in a dead tree alongside the road on the way to Fairbanks. He has peeled off the bark. Next he will sand it and apply a coat of varnish or shellac. It may end up as a mailbox post, or a lampstand, or who knows what.

Life in the park is different and nearly every day brings new challenges—especially for me, as I am always just a little frightened.

Six

Who's There?

Campground hosts get knocks on the door at all hours for a variety of reasons.

Knock, knock.

"Hi, what can I do for you?"
"Do you have any matches we could use?"
"Sure."
"I feel so silly to have forgotten matches."
"Don't. We get so many requests for matches that we keep a supply on hand."
"Thanks."
"You're welcome."

Knock, knock.

"Yeah, I'm really embarrassed, but do you have some forks we could use? We forgot to bring eating utensils."

"How about a knife, or some spoons too?"

"No, just some forks will do."

"Not a problem. Here you go."

Knock, knock.

"Hello."

"Hi. We are going out on the bus into the park tomorrow, and my camera battery is dead. Could you charge my camera for me?"

"Yes, but only when our generator is running. We can only run the generator between eight and ten a.m. and between four and eight p.m."

"Could I leave it now, and pick it up after eight?"

"Sure."

"Oh, that will be great. Thanks so much."

"You are very welcome."

Knock, knock.

"Hello."

"Hello. We just wanted to ask some questions about the park."

"Great! One of our favorite things to do is to talk about this park."

"Do you ever see any wildlife in the campground?"

"Absolutely! We see moose, grizzly bears, wolves, lynx …"

"Right here in the campground?"

"Yes, when we arrived here this season, we thought it was grizzly bear central."

"Really?"

"Really."

Two hours later, the same man pounds on our door. "Please, come right away," he gasped. "There are two grizzly bears across from our campsite and they are tearing up a tent or something. There is a lady in a trailer on that site, and she is screaming for help."

Dave runs out the door with the bear spray, while I get on the radio to call for bear technicians to come to our aid. They are nearby and soon they are at the site preparing to shoo the bears away, if they can. The techs have their guns ready just in case the bears decide they are not going to leave, or in case the bears charge the techs. The techs walk toward the bears, guns in hands, shouting at them. The bears decide that the fun is over and they leave. They tore up the lady's grass rug from in front of her trailer, but other than, that no damage is found.

The grizzly excitement is over; Dave and I are sitting by our campfire greeting campers out on their evening strolls. The skeptical camper stops by. "I thought you were exaggerating the wildlife the first time I talked to you," he said. "But now I realize that you were not."

"I could tell by the look on your face that you didn't believe me; so after you left I said to my husband, 'Cue the bears.'"

"Yeah, right. Like the Chevy Chase movie. Too funny." The skeptical camper walks away laughing.

A week or so later the same man is back at Savage River Campground with his son. "What are you guys doing back here?" I ask.

"We went farther out into the park to camp, but we had to come back here just to see if you could cue those bears again."

These two bears had fun playing with a campers grass rug, and were chased off by bear techs after scaring the campers.

Great Horned Owls are a frequent visitor to Savage Campground. These owls posed for a picture in a tree across from the host campsite.

Knock, knock.

"Hello."

"Do you have any graham crackers and marshmallows we could use? We only remembered to bring the chocolate for s'mores."

"Yes, we can help you."

"Thanks so much. The kids would have been so disappointed."

"You are most welcome."

Knock, knock.

"Hello."

"Hi, could you show me how to turn this thing on?" says a man with a camp stove in his arms.

"Sure."

He should have asked this question before he arrived in the wilderness, I thought.

Knock, knock.

"Good morning. How can I help you?"

"I've got a problem. I don't know if you can help me or not, but (with his voice breaking up with emotion) my dog died last night, and I don't know what to do with her."

"Oh, no. I'm so very sorry. I don't know what to tell you, but I will find out. I'll contact headquarters on the park radio and get right back with you."

"Savage River to Dispatch. Savage River to Dispatch…"

"Go ahead, Savage River."

"We have a camper whose dog died in the night, and he wants to know what he can do with the body."

"We'll check and get back with you, Savage River."

"Dispatch to Savage River."

"Go ahead, Dispatch."

"Yeah, we checked and he can't bury the dog in the park. He can go anywhere outside the park and dig a hole in the ditch and bury the dog."

"Are you kidding me? That's the answer: dig a hole in the ditch?"

"He can't bury the dog in the park."

"Okay. Ten-four, Dispatch."

"Dave, I am not going to tell that man to bury his dog in the ditch!"

"Let's give him the number of that nice veterinarian we saw. She will have a better solution."

After hearing what we found out for him, the man said he had a reservation at the main campground that tonight and he would call the vet as soon as he reached Riley Creek Campground and had use of his cell phone again.

The next day, Dave and I headed into the main camp to do our laundry and visit with our friends, the hosts at Riley Creek. Dennis told us that he talked to the man whose dog had died. The vet told him the same thing dispatch told us. When he called the humane society in Fairbanks, they offered to put the dog in the dumpster behind their building anytime. Nice.

So, Dennis did a really kind thing. He took his shovel and went with the guy to find a suitable burial spot outside the park. They went out Stampede Road near where they run dogsleds and dug a hole as deep as they could, and gave her a burial. Thanks, Denny.

Knock, knock.

"Hello."

"Hi, could you show us how to get our awning to come out?"

"Sure, be right with you."

Knock, knock.

"Hello. What can I do for you?"

"I need a wake-up call in the morning because I am supposed to catch the bus at seven a.m. and I'm afraid I will oversleep."

"Well, since there are no working phones here, a call is out of the question. What if we loan you an alarm clock?"

"That would be great. Thanks so much."

"Not a problem. We don't want you to miss your bus."

Knock, knock.

"What time is it?" I asked Dave. We were in bed.

"I don't know. Maybe two or three in the morning."

I stumbled to the door. In front of me are a man and a woman. "Hello."

"We were hiking in the park, and got lost. When we finally got headed in the right direction and got back to the road there were no more buses. We have been hiking since about noon yesterday. What we need is a ride back to McKinley Village, where we are staying."

"Oh, my goodness! Of course, I will give you a ride. Just let me get some clothes on, and I will be right with you."

As we pile into the truck, I wonder why I told Dave to go back to sleep and I'd give these people a ride. One of us must always remain in the park because we were on duty.

So, I was driving in the dark, the headlights of the truck providing the only light for at least twelve miles. I prayed I wouldn't hit a moose. As we drove out of the campground, the couple informed me there was another couple with them. This pair was waiting at the bus stop because they were too exhausted to walk any further. We stopped and picked them up; I could see how exhausted they were by their movements.

When everyone was seated and buckled, we made introductions all around, and the first couple shared water they had gotten at our campsite with the other two. "I'm sorry, I didn't even think about offering you anything to eat or drink," I said.

"That's okay. There is a room where we are staying that is open 24/7 with coffee, sandwiches, and cookies provided."

"Where exactly are you staying at McKinley Village?"

"At the elder hostel."

"Are you kidding me? So, tell me how you got stranded in Denali Park."

"We have hiked before and we have a GPS, so we rode the bus to the Savage Loop Trailhead and got off there to begin our hike. The plan was to hike to the top of Mt. Margaret, follow the ridge, and come down at Primrose Pass where we would catch a bus back to town. We made a wrong turn somewhere and by the time we realized it, we were way off course. We finally came across some hikers who gave us water and directed us to the park road. By the time we made it back to the park road, the last bus had already left. We had no choice but to keep walking. We thought if we could make it back to the Savage Loop Trailhead there would be a telephone, but when we finally made it that far, there was no telephone. We could see the park radio inside the security shed, and we thought about breaking a window to access it, but decided against it. We were afraid of being attacked by animals, and considered sleeping in the bathrooms until morning, but decided to keep walking, even though one of the ladies had hurt her knee and we were all tired and ached all over. We felt we needed to get to a place where there were people to ask for help. We have been walking now for about fourteen hours."

"Wow! That's some story."

"We are very grateful to you for giving us a ride."

"That is not a problem at all. I surely couldn't leave you out in the cold all night, could I?"

As I drive through the main camp at Riley Creek, a few street lights give us visual aid, but after getting on the highway it gets very dark again. I am driving slowly because I am afraid I will hit a moose, but I am also afraid that if a truck comes up behind us going fast, that could be a disaster too. The speed limit is 65 mph; so I force myself toward 50 mph and keep my eyes peeled on the road ahead. It's about twenty miles from camp to McKinley Village. When we arrive at the elder hostel, the lost hikers have difficulty stretching their sore muscles to get out of the truck.

I made the reverse trip, wishing the sun would come up so I didn't have to make the drive all the way home in the dark. The sun must have heard my request because it began to get light out by the time I neared Riley Creek. I was fully awake by the time I returned to the trailer, so I made coffee and got ready for the day. By midmorning though, I was thinking about a nap, when Dave said, "One of your late-night callers left a cell phone in the truck."

"Oh, no." Back in the truck I went—I hated driving that big monstrosity. When I reached McKinley Village, I explained the whole story to the man at the desk and told him that the people would not come looking at his lost and found for the cell phone; he would have to find them. I left my cell phone number with him.

A few days later, when we were off duty and had driven to the main camp at Riley Creek, I was able to access my cell phone messages. I learned that they did get their phone back. They will have stories to tell when they get home—and so will I.

Knock, knock …

Seven

Working with Law Enforcement

AMY O'CONNOR, A LAW ENFORCEMENT OFFICER IN Denali National Park and Preserve, is connected in spirit to those who passed this way many years ago. Amy and Mike O'Connor met while working in the park, fell in love, and were married in the amphitheater in Savage River Campground in August 2008. The Mike and Amy love story is reminiscent of Lena and Johnny Howard (see chapter eleven) who also fell in love while working together at Savage Camp. Frances Erickson (see chapter eleven) believes the spot where Jenny Creek meets Savage Fork is a special place where magical things can happen because that is where she met her husband while he was a wrangler at Savage Camp.

Mike and Amy live in one of the historic houses built by Civilian Conservation Corps workers in 1938.[1] I found an old photo of a park ranger in front of the same house with his dog. I couldn't resist taking a picture of Amy in the same spot with her dog Yetti.

...UNDER THE ABLE LEADERSHIP OF FRANKLIN G. FOX, PROJECT MANAGER, THE CCC CAMP IN MT. MCKINLEY NATIONAL PARK IS MAKING SPLENDID PROGRESS. IN LESS THAN FOUR WEEKS TIME A TENT VILLAGE HAS BEEN ERECTED NEAR PARK HEADQUARTERS, CONSISTING OF 60 TENTS HOUSING 210 MEN. PORTABLE BUILDINGS WERE ERECTED AND ARE USED FOR THE DINING ROOM, INFIRMARY, OFFICE AND THE LIKE.

TWO BASEMENTS HAVE BEEN EXCAVATED AND CONCRETE IS READY TO POUR FOR ONE OF THE RESIDENCES TO BE CONSTRUCTED AT PARK HEADQUARTERS. A NEW ROAD HAS BEEN BUILT LEADING TO THE PROPOSED SITE OF THE NEW DOG KENNEL LOCATION. OVER FOUR MILES OF ROADSIDE CLEAN-UP WORK HAS BEEN ACCOMPLISHED IN WHICH DEAD TREES AND SHRUBBERY HAVE BEEN REMOVED. TWELVE HUNDRED FEET OF FOUR-INCH PIPE HAVE BEEN LAID FOR THE WATER SYSTEM.

EVERY EFFORT WILL BE MADE TO CARRY OUT THE PROPOSED WORKING PROGRAM THIS SEASON IN SPITE OF THE FACT THAT THE CCC CONTINGENT DID NOT ARRIVE AT THE PARK UNTIL MAY 29.

...TWO AIR FLIGHTS IN HAKON CHRISTENSEN'S PLANE WERE MADE BY VISITORS ON SUNDAY EVENING. THE TRIPS WERE MADE FROM SAVAGE RIVER AIRFIELD TOWARD THE MOUNTAIN AND AROUND THE PARK.

Fairbanks Daily News-Miner,
"CCC Camp At M'McKinley Pk. August 1"
July 1, 1937

One of my first contacts with Amy involved some campers who broke the rules. Early one morning, as I was doing my rounds, I heard people having a very good time. Turning the corner and getting a view of the happy campers I saw a campsite cluttered with coolers, camp chairs, dishes, food, and women. They were busy having breakfast and the smells were heavenly. After wishing them a good morning, I moved on. They were not breaking any rules at that time because, although there were coolers and food around, the campers were there in possession of them. In an effort to protect both visitors and animals, campground hosts must keep constant vigilance to make sure that food is not where animals have access to it. Animals should not look to visitors for food—or as food!

About an hour later, there was a knock on the door of our trailer.

"Hi, Amy."

"Hi, Val. What do you know about site twenty-one?"

"I know that when I walked by there about an hour ago they were having a good time eating breakfast and the site was a cluttered mess."

"I need you to come with me now."

"No problem."

The site looked pretty much as it had earlier—except minus people. The campfire was still burning. Yikes!

"Will you get some water to put out this fire?" said Amy.

"Yes," I said, even as I wondered where I'd find any since there was no water running in the park yet and our trailer was out of water. Well, Aquafina it is. I grabbed a large bottle of water and ran back to the site. Thankfully, one Aquafina was enough to extinguish the fire.

Ranger Amy O'Connor with her sled dog Yetti in front of the historic ranger residence in Denali Park and Preserve 2009.

RANGER'S CABIN, McKINLEY PARK

An unknown ranger in front of his residence built by the Civilian Conservation Corps workers in 1938.

Photo courtesy of the Candy Waugaman collection.

"We have to confiscate this stuff. Will you help me load the coolers into the back of the patrol car?" said Amy.

"Sure."

The coolers were the large plastic ones and they were full of food and alcohol. With each of us taking one end, we could lift and carry them okay, but hoisting them into the back of the car took muscle. When both coolers were in the back of the vehicle, Amy looked down at her uniform pants and saw they had grime from the bottom of the coolers on them.

"Look at my pants! And I just got them back from the cleaners."

Brushing them off didn't do much, and we still had work to do; so we finished confiscating the remaining goods.

Amy said, "I think we will store this stuff in the food locker, where it should have been in the first place. I am going to leave them a note to notify them their things have been confiscated, and that they need to contact law enforcement to get them back. They will contact you, you can contact us on the park radio, and we will come out to talk with them and return their things. When you talk to them, do not tell them you know where their stuff is. Just say that you were told to contact law enforcement, and law enforcement will return their things."

"Okay, got it."

Much later that day, tired and hungry campers returned to their campsite after a full day of rafting the Nenana River. Much to their surprise they had no food or beverages to relieve their hunger and thirst. They headed for the campground host site.

"We just got back to our campsite and found this note saying that our things have been confiscated."

"I'll contact law enforcement and let them know that you're back."

An hour or so later—about 8 o'clock in the evening, the campers returned to our trailer. "Where is law enforcement? We want our stuff back. We have nothing to eat or drink."

Dave and I hesitated to contact dispatch again. "Law enforcement will be here as soon as they can. They are probably busy on another call. We notified them; they'll be here soon."

By 9 o'clock, the campers were very angry. They had had no supper. So, we contacted dispatch again.

When law enforcement finally met with the campers, it was 10 o'clock and it was not a pleasant experience. The campers finally did get their food back, along with about $300 worth of tickets. The biggest violation was leaving the campfire burning.

The next day, the park-cleaning crew came to our site to tell us they had just seen some grizzly bears heading into the campground. We rushed out to inform the campers so they were aware of the potential danger. Dave said, "I think our violators are down by the river. I'm going down there to be sure they are okay."

As I waited for Dave to return, a truck pulled into our host site. The people were very excited as they reported, "Some bears just walked onto our site. We left our picnic table and got into our truck. The bears walked past our truck and headed down the road toward the river.

I was worried about Dave and the women, but soon my fears were relieved when I saw them walking up the road from the river. They didn't even see the bears. The ladies had had enough of fines and bears and they soon packed up and left. I hurried down to check their site, and it was spotlessly clean.

When Amy is on duty, she drives through Savage River Campground and stops by our site for a campground update. Walking from our campsite toward the park road one day, I saw Amy driving into the campground. She stopped the car and rolled down her window.

"Hi, Amy."

"Hello."

"You are white as a sheet. What's the matter?"

"I just had a very unusual traffic stop."

"What happened?"

"Well, I came up behind a car headed out into the park. The car was weaving back and forth, so I followed it. It stopped suddenly and I almost rear-ended it because the brake lights did not come on. I thought maybe the driver was drunk or on drugs or something, so I lit her up and pulled her over. When I got to the driver's door, the woman seemed extremely nervous as she searched for her driver's license and registration. She was fumbling around without much success in finding her documents; so I finally asked her why she was so nervous.

"'There's a grizzly bear right behind you,' she said.

"I slowly turned and, sure enough, there was a grizzly bear just a few feet away. The bear seemed to be sizing me up, so I pulled out my service revolver because I thought I might have to shoot it. The lady asked if I wanted to get in her car. I told her that normally I would not get in someone's car but this was an unusual situation. So, avoiding any sudden moves, I slowly moved to the back door of the car and got in. Eventually the bear wandered off. I told the lady to get her brake lights fixed, and we both moved on—but I guess I am still a little shaken. I have never been that close to a bear before."

"Wow! I guess you can chalk that one up on your list of experiences. I wonder why the lady didn't tell you right away about the bear, instead of looking for her documentation."

"I don't know what she was thinking, but I am relieved the bear didn't decide to have me for lunch," said Amy.

Mike and Amy demonstrated their love for the park, the people, and the wildlife by their devotion to their duties. Working with them helped build our knowledge and enhanced our experience. They built a relationship with us as coworkers and as park conservators, and always made us feel as though we were an important part of a bigger picture of dedication to the safety of all concerned.

Eight

People of the Present

CAMPGROUND HOSTING IN DENALI PARK AND PRESERVE is an opportunity to meet people from across the globe while they stop briefly to encounter the wild. The most important duty of a campground host is to be out in the park talking with people, and thereby avoiding problems that may arise later. While chatting with the campers about the importance of securing their food supply, making sure campfires are out, and other rules, they often offer up their own stories about where they are from and what brought them to this location. Visitors to the park remark that they feel an energy and aura that draws them back. The park was established to protect the environment and the animals so that visitors to the area could enjoy the experience offered by this place.

May

We first met Reiner when he came to the campground-host site asking where he could leave his car while he went backpacking out in the bush for a while. As Dave and I were not aware at the time that the rule was for backpackers to park their vehicles near Riley Creek and take the camper bus out into the park, we said he could park his car on our site. Dave took pictures of Reiner as he headed out for the backcountry, and wrote down Reiner's day of return so that if something happened and he did not return someone would search for him. Returning to our campsite one day, we found a note: "Dear hosts, Thank you for your great hospitality! Reiner." How nice it was for him to leave a note. He was leaving to return to his home near Munich, Germany.

Mr. and Mrs. Jerry O. were from Montreal, Canada. They shoveled snow off roofs in Montreal the previous winter to earn money to visit Alaska. They flew to Anchorage and rented a van. His goal was to see a grizzly bear, and she wanted to see a wolf. They saw both before they left Savage River Campground. They told us to look them up if we were ever in Montreal.

Carlos and his wife stopped by our campfire to chat. She had climbed to the summit of Mt. McKinley in the 1990s, so they came to the park every year to camp on the anniversary of her climb. Ten people started up the mountain with her, but only seven made it to the summit. She experienced swelling of her hands and the roof of her mouth was burned by the reflection of the sun bouncing off the snow, but other than that, she had no problems. It took two weeks to reach the top, and only two days to return. On the way to the summit, you have to allow time for your body to acclimate to the higher elevations.

The same day we said good-bye to Carlos and his wife, we learned that two Japanese climbers were lost on the mountain and the search for them was called off. The view of the mountain changes for me then. It is no longer just beautiful and awe inspiring, it is imposing, unforgiving, hard, and cold.

June

Mayumi is backpack camping at Savage River Campground where the moose and the grizzly bears roam. She carries her tent, all of her food, utensils, and clothing on her back. It is cold at night; so the campfire that is kept burning at the campground-host site is a welcome beacon to campers. The food storage locker is located near the campground-host site, and when Mayumi arrives to store her food she is greeted by Remington Beagle, and invited to sit by the fire awhile. She describes herself as an ordinary office worker from Kawasaki, Japan. Mayumi is anything but ordinary. She has come to Alaska alone, to take part in a potlatch ceremony. Mayumi asks, "Do you know what a potlatch is?"

"I have heard the term before—isn't it some kind of native ceremony?"

"Yes. The Tlingits in Sitka built a totem pole in honor of Michio Hoshino, and the potlatch was the ceremony celebrating the raising of the totem. Do you know Michio Hoshino?"

"No, who is he?"

"He is a famous Japanese photographer. He is famous for his photographs of Alaska. Some of his photographs are displayed at the University of Alaska Fairbanks Museum. I admire him a great deal, and so I wanted to come to his potlatch, and then visit all of the places in Alaska he photographed. He was recently killed in Russia while photographing grizzly bears in Siberia. After the totem raising, I was also invited to take part in a sweat lodge ceremony which is a spiritual experience."

"Tell us more about your journey. Where did it start, and where have you been?"

"I flew from Japan to Vancouver, Canada; from there to Prince Rupert Sound and then to Sitka for the ceremonies. Then I went to Juneau, Skagway, Whitehorse, Fairbanks, and now I am here at Denali."

"And you did all of this by yourself. Aren't you scared staying in a tent with bears all around?"

"Yes, I am somewhat scared, but I went through the backpack training at the Wilderness Access Center. I am very careful to follow the rules, and I believe that I will be alright."

Passing Mayumi's campsite the next day, the neatness of the site is noticeable and causes me to reflect that Mayumi is as precisely manicured as her campsite. She is pretty and petite and looks about twenty years old although she says she is forty. She is not at her campsite during the day because she is out in the park hiking or exploring, getting the best out of every moment of her great adventure. At the end of the day, Mayumi appears again at the campfire to tell us what she has seen. "I saw a wolf on my bus trip, and when I got back to camp I saw a marmot. I was able to get a view of the mountain, and I just had a wonderful day."

Since Mayumi has sparked our interest, I do a little research on Michio Hoshino and am lucky enough to find a copy of Hoshino's Alaska at a local gift shop. Just as Mayumi is no ordinary office worker, Michio Hoshino is no ordinary photographer. His photographs are compelling because each one tells a story. White on white polar bears on pack ice, an aerial view of migrating caribou showing well-worn routes of travel, cotton grass near a pond with reflected cotton clouds above, a tiny ground squirrel in wild flowers against a background of a massive valley and mountains.

A day later, Mayumi appeared, ready to depart. "I didn't want to leave without saying good-bye, and to thank you once again for the warm cookies you brought me. I have something for you—it is a piece of the rope used to raise Michio's totem pole."

"Oh, my! What a lovely thought—but I cannot possibly take this from you."

"No. You must take it. You must."

"Mayumi, you have already given me a gift by introducing us to Michio Hoshino and his work. He is amazing and wonderful and I would never have known about him if not for you."

"Please, take it. Please."

"I am very honored by this gift. Each time I look at this, I will think of Michio Hoshino and you. Thank you."

"Here comes my bus. I must go."

"Good-bye Mayumi."

"Good-bye."

July

We met a lovely lady named Margaret who was supervising a group of students. She had a problem. When she checked in at the mercantile she was told they had group site B, but that site was already occupied. Checking the group site schedule, I saw that they should actually be on site A.

"We come here with a school group every year, and we hate site A. It is just too rocky."

"How do you feel about group site C? "

"We would love C! Can you do that for us?"

"Sure."

Problem solved.

A couple hours later, we saw Margaret again. "One of

A wolf by the side of the park road near the Savage River Campground. Wolves are not only beautiful but very intelligent.

Boreal Owl found by Margaret's school group. This owl is small and nocturnal which accounts for its discovery at near midnight.

my girls left her hiking boots where we stayed last night. The only shoes she has are some flimsy canvas ones that will not do for hiking. Do you know where there is a place nearby we could go to find hiking boots?"

"What size does she wear? I twisted my knee in the spongy tundra and will not be using my hiking boots anytime soon."

The boots fit. Problem solved.

A short time later, two of the girls from group site C approached our campfire and told Dave that on their way back from the bathroom they saw something go into the woods so they followed it. When it stopped and stood on its hind legs they realized it was a bear. Yikes! Dave took this opportunity to reinforce what one is supposed to do when you see a bear, and more importantly what to do when the bear sees you. Problem avoided.

The next night, Dave decided to stir things up at C camp. He tells the kids about a lynx we often see late at night and early in the morning. So, a lynx hunt it is! Off they went with cameras, binoculars, and walkie-talkies. What they found were two Boreal owls. Margaret and one of the girls returned to the host site to share their find. On their way back, they see the elusive lynx and get an awesome photo before the lynx decides to leave. When they knock on the campground-host door, Dave is out somewhere in the park and I am in my pajamas with wet hair.

"Would you like to come see some Boreal owls?" they ask.

"Sure. I'll just throw on a jacket over my pajamas and be right with you."

Nearing midnight, I find myself walking back to the trailer alone. I breathe deeply, taking in the woodsy smells.

I look at the mountains that circle the camp and pause to recollect:

> "I WENT TO THE WOODS BECAUSE I WISHED TO LIVE DELIBERATELY, TO FRONT ONLY THE ESSENTIAL FACTS OF LIFE, AND SEE IF I COULD NOT LEARN WHAT IT HAD TO TEACH, AND NOT, WHEN I CAME TO DIE, DISCOVER THAT I HAD NOT LIVED. I DID NOT WISH TO LIVE WHAT WAS NOT LIFE, LIVING IS SO DEAR, NOR DID I WISH TO PRACTICE RESIGNATION, UNLESS IT WAS QUITE NECESSARY. I WANTED TO LIVE DEEP AND SUCK OUT ALL THE MARROW OF LIFE, TO LIVE SO STURDILY AND SPARTAN-LIKE AS TO PUT TO ROUT ALL THAT WAS NOT LIFE, TO CUT A BROAD SWATH AND SHAVE CLOSE, TO DRIVE LIFE INTO A CORNER, AND REDUCE IT TO ITS LOWEST TERMS.

Henry David Thoreau

There was a knock on the door at 7 a.m. Campers had locked their keys in the car and they had tickets for the Eielson Bus at 8 a.m. A radio call is made to dispatch for vehicle lockout assistance. The campers decide to catch the bus even though their cameras, binoculars, and sunscreen are in the car. The lockout-assistance crew arrives about 2 p.m. proving that everything takes longer in Alaska. When the campers returned around suppertime they were very happy because they thought they would have to call Fairbanks for a wrecker and that would be pricey.

Mr. and Mrs. Nord C have traveled from Connecticut on a motorcycle. They were in Haines Junction last week and woke up to six inches of snow one morning.

Lately, it has been rain, rain, and more rain. Add to that cold temperatures at higher elevations and the rain is white. Some Aussie tourists tell us that this is not cold. In Brisbane, Australia, it's cold.

"You know it is cold when you step out of doors, hug yourself with your arms while shifting from one foot to the other and shivering." They demonstrate.

I said, "That must be the Brisbane shuffle."

We love the Aussies. They are so genuine. They are making fun of the way Americans talk.

"Hey, we don't talk funny—you talk funny."

They tell us they came to Alaska because it is summer here. Amazing!

August

Jennifer and Bonnie are schoolteachers in a little Yup'ik Eskimo village called Kwigillingok. On the map it looks as if it is right on the ocean, but it is actually a mile or two inland on the Kwigillingok River. You can get there only by plane or boat.

Jennifer teaches math and science to junior high and high school students. Bonnie teaches third and fourth graders language development and academics. When Jennifer completed her college degree, there were no jobs near her home; so she decided to apply for jobs in places where she had always wanted to visit. Bonnie was in a transition in her life; she didn't want to work in a big city, so Alaska became her choice. However, the question is not why they came—rather it is why do they stay?

There is snow on the ground today and the ladies are preparing their breakfast on a butane camp stove. It is like cooking on an aerosol can with four little wings protruding from the top to set your pan on. They are having biscuits and gravy. Bonnie works on the gravy and Jennifer is stirring up the biscuits. When Bonnie gets the gravy boiling, they drop the biscuit batter into it; so it is more like dumplings than biscuits. Before they started to cook the main course, they heated water and made coffee and tea. They are drinking that while they wait for their biscuits and gravy. They have to drink it in a hurry if they want it hot because the air is so cold. Bonnie is sipping tea and scraping snow off the table to clear a place for eating.

What remarkable people they are; and I am sure they are remarkable teachers because they know that a key to facilitating learning is building relationships. These ladies obviously care a great deal for their students as demonstrated by the sacrifices they willingly make for them and the loving way they talk about them. They stay because they love what they do, and they love who they do it for. They are loading their backpacks for a hike up Mt. Margaret to see if they can watch any Dall sheep up close. What else can you do in the snow? I'm thinking maybe browsing at gift stores.

Jen and Bob are from Cambridge, England. They are retired and have traveled ever since. They spent two and a half years in Australia and have visited New Zealand, South Africa, Antarctica, Europe, and much of the U.S. Their perspective and worldview make them interesting to talk with. They like the British royalty and system of government and believe it is preferable to ours. They respect the queen, and they like Prince Charles, William, and Harry. Diana was approved of at first, but later she became a "loose cannon." Fergie is a tart, but she never pretended to be anything but a tart.

Planning for this trip took time. They booked their rental motorhome a year ago online. They paid for it ahead of time and thought they had a pretty good deal—until they actually got to Alaska and picked it up. When they rented the motorhome that's what they got and nothing else. No dishes, pots and pans, sheets on the bed, or towels. So, the first stop was to pick up the necessities. The toilet leaks and Bob is hoping they can return the vehicle before other problems surface. Our good wishes go with them as they leave.

Luca and Stefania are from Rome, Italy. Luca works in the travel business and Stefania works for a company that advises the Italian government on environmental issues. They kayaked in Prince William Sound and a whale swam under their kayak. Yikes. They come to our campfire every night and share their daily adventures with us. When they leave we feel a loss.

Italians are so polite and cultured. Although it is true that they have had thousands of years to get the whole culture thing right, Americans often seem crude in contrast. Like the American guy in the tent across from us with a device that makes a noise like someone expelling gas. He has the fart machine hung in a tree by the road. He evidently has a remote control for this and sits in a chair by his campfire waiting for his next victim. When people walk by they will abruptly be serenaded by sounds of expelled gas. Some stop and look around, some look with blame at each other, and others have no reaction. Actually it is quite childish. I wonder if it counts as excessive noise after ten p.m.

Talk about excessive noise after ten…one night when Dave was walking around the campground, checking for any food that might have been left out, he heard some noises coming from a tent. He stopped because at first he thought the person was in pain due to all of the moaning he heard, but then he realized it was some kind of religious experience because the female kept shouting, "Oh, God! Oh my, God!" The campers at that end of the campground gave the couple a smile and a nod the next morning.

Jess is a marine biologist. She works out of Anchorage on fishing boats doing research. She is sometimes stationed in Dutch Harbor, Alaska. Jess is camping by herself. She went for a hike today and fell in a bog. To make matters worse, it has been raining steady ever since. As Dave walked by her campsite, he saw that she was trying to dry her clothes by her campfire; so now she has wet and smoky clothes. Dave had Jess bring her wet things to our trailer and we put them on drying racks for the night. We gave her some dry clothes to wear and a couple of dry blankets. Jess says she will be fine for the night.

Responding to a knock on the door, I find a lovely young woman with blonde hair and blue eyes. With a lilt in her voice she inquires, "I was wondering if there is a ranger program in the park tonight, and if there is one, could you tell me where it is?" I gladly give her the information and point her in the right direction. Roisin is from Spiddal, Ireland. Her family owns a caravan park there. (That's what we call a campground in the U.S.)

After a very cold night, Roisin approaches again to ask if they sell warm clothing at the Wilderness Access Center. "We put every piece of clothing that we have with us on last night and we still nearly froze. We are going from here to Igloo and then to Wonder Lake, and we thought we would take the shuttle to the Wilderness Access Center, get some more warm clothes, and then take the bus to the Igloo Campground. Do you know how cold it got last night?"

"My thermometer said twenty-six degrees Fahrenheit at six this morning. Two young women backpacking alone in the wild—you are courageous."

Pointing to her friend, Roisin said, "Sorcha is more courageous than me. Last night was her first night to sleep in a tent. We are teachers from Ireland, here on sabbatical in the United States. We have been in the state of Washington and decided that we should take the opportunity to see Alaska while we were so close. It is so expensive to get to Alaska from Ireland. They both wish they had planned better for cold weather.

Today is wedding day! We have been working with Amy and Mike O'Connor all season, and today they will be married in the park. Savage River Campground is the perfect place for their wedding. Pre-ceremony wine and cheese are served at group site A allowing the guests to mingle and view the mountain. Next, the guests walk to the amphitheater for the wedding ceremony. Bridesmaids are in variations of the same color dress and carry bouquets of fall flowers. The day would not be complete without Yetti and Sushi. Yetti is their white sled dog and Sushi is a Newfoundland—pure black and huge. Amy is beautiful out of uniform and in her wedding dress, and the groom is handsome and nervous. Perfect!

September

The National Park Service holds a road lottery every year. People buy chances to drive into the park in their private vehicles. Private vehicles are usually not allowed past the checkpoint at Savage River Bridge. If your ticket is lucky and you win, you are allowed a day to drive as far out on the park road as you wish.

Mike and Amy get married in the amphitheater in Savage Campground.

This continues for four days, and some folks are lucky enough to win more than one day. Many of these people camp at Savage River because it gives them a 12.8 mile advantage into the park at the start of the day. Our boss says that we should encourage all campers to leave by check-out time on the last day; then Dave and I must leave and lock the gate behind us.

I think about the day we arrived at Savage River Campground, with its locked gate and snow on the ground. I remember how Dave and I invaded the space that had been the domain of the animals all winter; I thank the animals for graciously sharing their habitat with us all summer. And now, we return it to them…until next year.

Nine

Remington Beagle

OUR ADVENTURES TRAVELLING TO AND WORKING IN ALASKA were shared by our friend and companion Remington Beagle. He was most often the first to greet anyone coming onto our campsite. As people stopped to pet Remington it was an opportunity to strike up a conversation. As in most any other job communication is the key to good campground hosting. If you build rapport with campers it is much easier when you have to request that they comply with rules. So Remington was a big help to us in establishing good relations with our customers.

Each day that we were on duty we would walk the whole campground many times. I started my day at 7:00 a.m. with a walk through the campground. At this time of the day there was a lot of activity because people were eating breakfast and getting ready for their activities for the day. My next walk about would usually be about 9:00 a.m., and Remington always accompanied me on this second trip around the campground. This hike took longer than the first because Remington needed to stop and sniff along the way. If he saw another dog on a campsite, the next trip through the campground he would be looking for the dog before we reached that site again.

One day as Remington and I traversed the campground we rounded a curve in the road and came face to face with a huge cow moose. I'm not sure which of us was the most startled. I was very scared because we learned that more people are injured by moose every year in the park than by grizzly bears. Moose will trample you, and especially if there is a dog involved because moose look at any dog as though it is a wolf and wolves are a major danger to moose because they eat their young and weak. So after a quick intake of air, I started pulling back on Remington's leash and speaking softly to the moose. As I backed up so did Remington – he did not make a sound, but was fixated on the moose. I was backing toward the trees at the edge of the road thinking that maybe I could escape a trampling by getting behind a tree, but what about Remington? He continued to slowly and silently back up with me when all of a sudden the moose darted into the woods on the opposite side of the road and away from us. I believe that if Remington had not been silent we probably would have been attacked by that moose. He rarely barks which is unusual for a beagle, but I was thankful that he chose this time to be silent.

I enjoyed working in the park during the early hours of the day and into the afternoon when Dave would take over the hosting duties. Dave walked the park or stayed by our campfire until the park was quiet and we assumed the campers were in bed for the night. During his nightly excursions around the park he regularly saw a lynx. Snowshoe hares were plentiful in the park and that is a favorite food for a lynx.

A Note from Remington Beagle:

Val and I went for a walk after supper today. I should say that Val went for a walk, and I went for a sniff. I am very happy to be on a sniff, and I am wagging my tail and sniffing along. Let's see...that's snowshoe hare, snowshoe hare, the neighbor's dogs, red squirrel, human, ptarmigan...this is so much fun!

We are walking from our campsite out toward the park road, and on our way we pass the big park bulletin board where information about the park and schedules for interpretive programs are posted. The bulletin board is enclosed with glass and has a nice shake-shingled roof. It was lying on the ground for a while, because the supporting posts had rotted, and a good wind blew it down. When it was lying on the ground I would chuckle to myself to see humans bending over to read the stuff on the ground. Anyhow, no one is at the bulletin board today as we walk and sniff on by.

We are casually moving along toward the exit of the campground when all of a sudden I smell a smell I have never smelled before. This is so different, and so fresh, and so wild, that ignoring the rules for dogs to keep off of trails and out of the woods, I instinctively head toward the enticing aroma.

"Remington! You can't go in there."

Lynx that was found by Remington Beagle and waited by the side of the road for a picture 2009.

I never tired of the view of Mt. McKinley from the Savage River Campground.

"ARE YOU KIDDING ME? THIS SCENT IS REALLY SOMETHING—I NEED TO KEEP GOING."

RIGHT ABOUT NOW VAL NOTICES THAT MY HACKLES ARE UP. SHE KNEELS DOWN AND LOOKS IN THE DIRECTION I AM SNIFFING.

"YIKES! IT'S A LYNX," SHE SAYS.

HER HUMAN EYES ARE BETTER THAN MINE. I CAN'T SEE THE THING, BUT I SURE KNOW IT'S THERE. BEFORE I KNOW WHAT HAS HIT ME, SHE HAS PICKED ME UP AND IS HURRYING BACK TO THE TRAILER. WELL, THAT WAS A SHORT WALK!

"DAVE, REMINGTON FOUND A LYNX. I'M GOING BACK TO GET A PICTURE. WANNA COME?"

"NO, YOU GO AHEAD. DO YOU REALLY THINK THAT THE LYNX IS GOING TO WAIT FOR YOU TO GET BACK WITH THE CAMERA?"

SURE ENOUGH, WHEN VAL GETS BACK TO THE SPOT—NO LYNX. SHE JUST HATES IT WHEN DAVE IS ALWAYS RIGHT. DOWN ON ONE KNEE SHE SCANS THE WOODS, TO NO AVAIL. TURNING TO HEAD BACK AND ADMIT FAILURE, SHE LOOKS ON THE OPPOSITE SIDE OF THE ROAD AND THERE HE IS! VAL IS ABLE TO GET HER PICTURE AND TRIUMPHANTLY RETURN TO CAMP WITH HER PRIZE. SHE GIVES ME ALL THE CREDIT, SAYING THAT SHE NEVER WOULD HAVE SEEN IT IN THE FIRST PLACE IF IT HADN'T BEEN FOR ME.

The ranger doing the interpretive programs told Dave that her program that evening was going to be on lynx. Dave told her that we have been seeing one or two different lynx in the campground nearly every night. Dave jokingly said he would try to get one to walk her way for her presentation. The ranger was just beginning her program when a lynx casually strolled the perimeter of the amphitheater behind her and then went off into the woods. When the program was over, Dave said to the ranger, "That'll be $20 for the lynx appearance."

The ranger laughed and said, "Tomorrow I'm doing a program at Riley Creek on grizzly bears. Can you get me a grizzly?"

"That'll be $50," said Dave.

Walking the park with Remington made me feel somewhat safer because I felt that he would alert me to approaching danger. I never really got over my fear, but the good thing was that I worked through it. I had a job to do and I just had to suck it up and do it – and I'm so glad that I did.

Ten

Reflections

THE BLUFF AT THE END OF THE CAMPGROUND WAS MY favorite. When I was out there all alone I felt an intimate connection with God. I felt as though I could reach out and touch the power of the universe. This gave me a sense of super awareness – there was a very strong connection with my surroundings. I felt a connection to the past and the people who came to this place before me.

Standing on that magical bluff my thoughts take me back to a time when there was a young Athabascan woman sitting by her fire near the bank of Jenny Creek. She was pleased to have the heavy iron pot her mate had been able to get in trade. Although no one from her family ever had any contact with outsiders, her spouse and some others would trade with natives of the south and the west coasts of Alaska who did have contact with Europeans and were thus able to get things like her cooking pot. The subarctic boreal forest in which the Athabascan's settled is surrounded by mountain ranges which made the interior difficult to penetrate by early explorers. The young couple living on the banks of Jenny Creek are part of a hearty group who learn. to adapt to this harsh climate while establishing a rich culture uniquely their own. These people lived mainly near rivers. The rivers were then and continue to be a source of food and travel. In the winter the frozen rivers become roads. In the summer months this small group will join with others to hunt, fish and gather, but when the harsh winter months come it is too difficult to provide for large groups, and so they split up and struggle for survival until the warm months of plenty return. Although her life was difficult in these winter months, she loved the memory of those nights when the sky was full of light. It seemed to her that the sky came alive with color starting with flowing movement of green and sometimes other colors would emerge in a natural light show of amazing proportions. As she sits by her fire watching the light she dreams of success in hunting, or of meeting up with family and friends in the spring.

Everyone in the group worked hard in this environment in order to get enough food just to stay alive – and they made use of every bit of what they harvested. When her mate killed a caribou, our young native wife would help to skin the animal, and every part of the animal was put to use. She would of course cook the meat for immediate consumption, and some was dried for future use. The bones and antlers were made into tools and weapons. The skin was used as clothing, bedding, and stretched over wood frames for shelter. Sometimes the skin was cut into strips called babiche and used to make snowshoes. This little family survived due to the animals they harvested as well as from other fruits of the land.

Her spouse knew that he was connected to the land and the animals not only physically, but spiritually. Although

[illegible] was complex, he essentially believed that
[illegible] and some inanimate ones have a spirit. His
[illegible] ht him that the spirits of men and animals
[illegible] and in the past men and animals had the
[illegible] with each other. Our hunter knew that relationships between men and animals were a key to survival, and he took care not to offend the spirits of the animals they relied on for food, clothing and shelter. Some animals had a stronger spirit than others such as the wolf, the bear, the caribou, and especially the wolverine. The spirit of an animal lived on after physical death, and those spirits had power. Our hunter took steps to avoid making the spirit of an animal angry, because if he angered the spirit of the animal he would not have luck in capturing the animal in the future. When the leader of this group went hunting he would look for a raven that might help him in his hunt. The raven would sometimes fly toward game, and if the hunter followed the sign he would be lucky in his hunt. His belief was that the ravens did this in order to get their share in what the hunter left behind. Ravens are still plentiful at Savage River Campground, and their raucous calls wake many a sleepy camper.

The harsh environment still causes people to band together as of old for protection and support. Grant Pearson was right - we do achieve our greatest feats when we work together. I left the comfort of my easy chair in a small tourist town and learned that I could meet the challenge of living in a place where the animals were plentiful, wild, and free. I faced up to a moose with my little dog and I am still here to tell the story. Grizzly bears passing through the campground were not uncommon. Lynx roamed like alley cats, and we saw wolves and more often signs of wolves in and around the camp. But the animals are only part of the story. It's the people of the present and the people of the past that have made a mark on our hearts and the hearts of so many others. They are the ones who have provided unforgettable memories of the journey.

Eleven

People of the Past

Bobby Sheldon

It was a man named Sheldon who was instrumental in getting the legislation passed to make this a park and preserve, but it was another Sheldon who was the driving force in making the original camp at Savage River a success.

One of the special people who left a legacy as he passed by Savage River was Robert E. "Bobby" Sheldon who managed the tourist camp at Savage River for seventeen years. He organized setting up the camp, tearing it down, and everything in between. If canvas needed repair, he was at the sewing machine. Frances Erickson, Sheldon's daughter, said of camp life, "You just did whatever needed doing."[1] Bobby led by example, and so the people who worked at the park followed his lead, happily switching hats whenever necessary, and even working long hours without extra pay.

Sheldon's ability to do whatever needed doing came from life experience. His mother died when he was only twelve years old, and when Bobby was fourteen his father decided to head for Alaska and the gold rush. He planned

Robert E. (Bobby) Sheldon at the sewing machine, and Johnny Howard helping. Lowell, Ted and Babe.

Photographs. UAF 2000-0126-00426[1].
University of Alaska Fairbanks.

to leave Bobby with an uncle, but Bobby said, "You're not leaving me with anybody. Wherever you go, I go."[2]

In 1897, they left on a steamship from Seattle for Skagway, Alaska. The trip was a risky one because "in those days they had no aids to navigation at all—no buoys, no lighthouses, no help of any kind. They blew their whistle and listened to the echo, and if they bumped into the bank, they pushed off and started out again…a good many of them didn't make it."[3]

Bobby and his dad planned to take the White Pass Trail[4] to the gold fields, but first they took jobs building the Brackett road up through the pass. However, the company constructing the road soon went bankrupt, and they were both out of work. Then Sheldon's father had a heart attack.

When he recovered, he decided to return to Oregon, and wanted Bobby to go with him. Bobby told his dad, "I left that country broke and I'm not going back the same way."[5] Fifteen-year-old Bobby Sheldon found himself alone in Skagway, Alaska. He needed to find a way to support himself. Since he had sold newspapers in Seattle, Washington, he bought Seattle newspapers for five cents, paid two cents each for shipping, then sold them for twenty-five cents each. Sometimes he would get fifty cents from big spenders. "It was the only communication we had with the United States…so there was no trouble making a living."[6]

In 1899, Sheldon learned of the death of his father in that same newspaper. He felt like he was truly alone, but later in life he would say, "When my father died he left me probably one of the largest estates that any boy was ever left. He left me the entire territory of Alaska in which to try to make a living, and I've been trying to collect on that estate ever since."[7]

In 1898, when Bobby was fifteen, he witnessed the shooting of Soapy Smith and Frank Reid on the dock at Skagway. He describes it as being "just like a play on the stage."[8] Sheldon relates that Soapy Smith was to Skagway what Al Capone was to Chicago. "Several preachers were soliciting funds in Skagway at the time, for instance, to start building churches, just like they are in Fairbanks today, and when the preacher would come along and ask for a collection, donations, contributions, Soapy would say, "Sure, you bet your life." He'd get $100 and throw it right in. The preacher would be very appreciative and go on his way. Soapy would say to one of his trusted lieutenants, "You follow that guy, and when you think he's got enough to make it worthwhile, why, bring it back."[9]

Jefferson Randolph Smith got the nickname Soapy because he ran a scam where he would wrap large and small denominations of bills in with bars of soap in view of a crowd of people and then offer the bars of soap for sale at $1.00 each.[10] No one ever got more than $5.00, and Soapy got rich. The businesspeople of Skagway felt that if something was not done about Soapy Smith their investments were lost.

When a miner came into town with a "poke" worth about $2,500 and was robbed by Soapy's men it precipitated action. They called a secret meeting on the wharf to decide what to do about Soapy. Soapy learned of the meeting, headed down to the docks with his Winchester on his shoulder, and was met by Frank Reid. "We couldn't hear what the men were saying...Soapy Smith whipped his rifle right down off his shoulder...toward Mr. Reid...he (Reid) jumped down off of the railing and grabbed the muzzle of that gun with his left hand to jerk it away from him, because it was pointed right at his middle...Soapy Smith pulled the trigger and the ball went right through his groin, and put him to his knees. Even on his knees Frank Reid was a tall man, a big man—even on his knees he was pretty near as big as Soapy Smith. But he held that gun away, while Soapy Smith was trying to jerk it back...In the meantime, he (Reid) reached in and got his .38 revolver, and fired three shots while this gun was being jerked back and forth."[11] One of Reid's bullets went through Soapy's heart. Reid died two weeks later. "Now, the sentiment against Soapy Smith was so strong that when they took his body out to the cemetery, they wouldn't bury his body in the cemetery and desecrate that hallowed ground."[12] They buried him outside the cemetery with a wooden board for a marker that read: "Jefferson Randolph Smith aged 38, died July the 8th 1898."[13] Frank

Reid received a very fine monument of Alaska granite, and it read: "He gave his life for the honor of Skagway."[14] Sheldon later used this life experience at Savage Camp by entertaining visitors with his eyewitness account.

Sheldon's talent for mechanics led him to work on steamships and pile-driving machines. He was recommended to General Wiles P. Richardson who was looking for a pile-driver crew to build a dock at Haines. Working together, Sheldon and Richardson became good friends. Sheldon later stated, "Every time he would come to Fairbanks, he would look me up and we would have a good party and celebrate the old days. He was a wonderful person, and this road from here to the coast is named for him."[15]

In 1905, Sheldon was employed as the night engineer for the Northwest Light and Power Company. While employed there he built Alaska's first automobile. He had heard about automobiles, but had never seen one. He built it for a girl he was courting. Another of her suitors had a handsome horse and buggy; so Sheldon felt he had to do something to compete. "He won first prize in the 4th of July parade for the most original entry,"[16] but he didn't win the girl. She married the guy with the horse and buggy.

In 1908, Sheldon moved to Fairbanks and "took over the power plant at Fairbanks for the Northern Commercial Company, and was the engineer operating that plant for five years."[17] While employed at Northern Commercial Company, Sheldon brought the first Model T Ford into Alaska. The "car had to come by rail to Seattle, and by boat to Skagway. Transported to Whitehorse, Yukon Territory by the new White Pass & Yukon Railroad (completed 1900) it followed the Gold Rush trail by boat down the Yukon past the famous mining town of Dawson, across

The Sheldon car – the first car in Alaska – is currently on display the antique car museum in Fairbanks, Alaska on loan from the University of Alaska Fairbanks.

the Alaska border into the Tanana River and smaller Chena River to Fairbanks."[18]

He was single, had a good job, and his plan was to have a lot of fun with the car. "There were only a few miles of wagon roads around Fairbanks. These were poorly located, undrained and unsurfaced."[19] He took a vacation and spent the time bringing his friends from areas outside of Fairbanks into town with his car. They could make the trip to town in about an hour, a trip that would otherwise take them a couple of days in a buckboard wagon pulled by horses. They insisted on paying Sheldon for the service which he did not want to accept, but they forced it on him. He made trips around the clock picking up folks and taking them back home. When the vacation was over, he ended up with $1,500. That's what made him think about the money that could be made in the automobile business.

Sheldon wanted to see if he could drive to the coast from the interior because at that time (1913) it took anywhere from twenty-eight to thirty-two days to get from Fairbanks to Seattle via riverboat, steamship, and overland travel. He decided to drive his Model T from Fairbanks to Valdez on the trail that Richardson was just beginning to improve. Sheldon chose a couple of strong men to be passengers and to help him if needed. They didn't have any spare parts for the car, and they strapped 40-gallon cans of gasoline to the running boards. They "jolted over rocks and tree roots and splashed through mud holes and shallow streams. Brush raked along the side of the car, and its occupants had to be alert to avoid being whipped in the face as branches slid past the windshield."[20] When they came to the Tanana River it was in flood stage so they tied planks to two poling boats and floated the car across. There were many tense moments getting the car on and off the planks, and keeping it steady while it floated across the river. When the car bogged down in mud, the passengers had to get out and push and pull the car along the treacherous route. In the Thompson Pass the road was little more than a "goat trail," and at one point a snow slide completely blocked their way. Their troubles were almost over as they neared Valdez, and then found that a bridge was out. With the help of his passengers, Sheldon got the Ford across the river and up a steep bank. They arrived in Valdez "at eleven o'clock Saturday night, August 2, 1913."[21]

On Monday, August 4, 1913, the Valdez Daily Prospector commented on the excursion: "It is believed that this automobile run will help greatly in getting road appropriation hereafter. It will also advertise Alaska among those numerous folks who think the territory is all ice and snow." Sheldon knew that he wouldn't be able to make it

back to Fairbanks alone, so he sold his car in V?
ordered another one. He purchased a bicycle and m..
way back up the Richardson trail alone back to Fairbanks.

As soon as his new Model T car arrived, Sheldon started
to build his transportation business, which was successful
for ten years. At one time, they had fifteen cars running
between Fairbanks and Valdez. As roads improved and more
cars were purchased, Sheldon also opened a repair garage
in Fairbanks. Business in transporting customers declined
when the railroad was extended from Seward to Fairbanks.
Then, as one business failed, other opportunities opened
up for Sheldon. "So, like a lot of people in Alaska who
made a failure of business, I finally got into politics."[22]

His first political victory was to be elected Road
Commissioner for the 4th Division. After four years, he
ran for the legislature, was elected, and went to Juneau for
the 1925 session. He was re-elected in 1926, and returned
for the 1927 session. After the United States purchased
Alaska in 1867, there was no formal government for 17
years. It was then defined by congress as a civil and judicial
district, and only made a territory in 1912.[23] It was this
territorial legislature that Robert E. (Bobby) Sheldeon
served in the 1920's. The territory was made a state in
January of 1959 and Sheldon also served in the House of
Representatives in the first state legislature. Sheldon lived
in the state of Washington when it was a territory. He was
three years old when Washington became a state. Then he
lived in Alaska when it was a territory, and later when it
became a state. He also served his community as postmaster
of Fairbanks for many years.

Sheldon was a risk taker, adventure seeker, and automobile lover. Just one hour after his wedding to Anna

Blondeau on August 20, 1922, he "was to go up against possible death in a crazy auto race which even gouging, kicking and biting were not barred and if anything happened to him he was going to leave Anna a rich widow. And, that he wasn't afraid is evidenced by the fact that he kept the undertaker right along with him, from the wedding to the finish of the grueling race, which he won, together with driver Ensley, their time being the same to the fraction of a second."[24] Anna Sheldon must have shared Bobby's attachment to autos and taking risks because she would later drive tourists to Chocolate Mountain in Mt. McKinley National Park and Preserve where the road was so narrow and dangerous that traffic could only go one way. Drivers had to be sure that everyone was up the road to its end before anyone started down. When Anna got to the end of the road, the tourists would ask to get out of the car before she turned it around.[25]

Bobby was willing to do almost anything to keep his guests entertained. He caught two bear cubs on Richardson Highway and brought them to Savage Camp—to the delight of visitors. When the season ended, however, he couldn't just leave the bears there; so, he submitted an article to the newspaper trying to "locate a person who will protect, love and zealously guard the two Alaskan grizzly bears now residing at Savage Camp. He stated that their keeper must treat the bears as one of their own family during the coming winter and release them to the company next summer -he's had no takers yet!"[26] The problem was solved when the Director of the National Parks facilitated giving the bears to the National Zoological Garden in Washington, D.C.

Leaving Fairbanks on the morning train, you arrive at the park station about 2 o'clock in the afternoon. There you are met by a string of Studebaker automobiles operated by the Mt. McKinley Tourist and Transportation Company. After your baggage has been loaded into a truck and you are comfortably seated in the car the ten-mile ride to the company's base camp at Savage River begins. After you have gone about two miles you come to the headquarters of Harry Karstens, superintendent of the Park. The group of log cabins set in the encircling mountains and surrounded by a heavy growth of spruce, presents a picturesque appearance. There you are asked to register in order that a record may be kept of all visitors into the park.

The rest of the ride to the camp is made over fine roads, and the automobile goes through rolling hills heavily wooded only to shoot out into the open country, giving at all times a pleasant variety to the trip. Always the high mountains of the great range stand out in relief.

Upon arrival at the camp you are pleasantly delighted; it is built in a sort of basin on a high plateau, and towering not far away are rugged peaks. Too, the appearance of the camp, so modern and clean is refreshing for out in the wilderness you did not expect anything like it. It is situated not far from the Savage River, and fresh running water is supplied at all times by a hydraulic ram. The main buildings, the kitchen, dining room and social hall, are connected.

THE CHEF, WILLIAM PHINN, HAS A WELL-MERITED REPUTATION FOR EXCELLENT COOKING. THE DINING ROOM HAS FOUR LONG TABLES, AND UNLIKE THE ORDINARY CAMP, CHAIRS ARE USED INSTEAD OF BENCHES. YOU SIT DOWN AT A TABLE THAT IS COVERED WITH SNOWY LINEN AND NAPKINS— ARTICLES SCARCELY LOOKED FOR IN THE WILDERNESS. THE SOCIAL HALL HAS A FINE FLOOR FOR DANCING AND ORTHOPHONIC VICTROLA. TABLES ARE PROVIDED FOR THOSE WHO CARE TO PLAY CARDS.

YOU REGISTER AS YOU WOULD AT ANY HOTEL AND ARE ESCORTED TO A TENT. THE TENTS ARE SET ALONG REGULAR STREETS AND EACH WILL HOUSE TWO PERSONS COMFORTABLY AS THEY ARE 10 FEET BY 12 FEET IN SIZE. TWO COTS ARE PLACED IN EACH; BOARD FLOORS AND FRAMES KEEP OUT THE MOISTURE. HOT WATER IS BROUGHT TO YOU IN THE TENT EACH MORNING. IT IS CAMPING DELUXE.

BACK OF THE MAIN GROUP OF BUILDINGS IS THE CORRAL IN WHICH 27 HORSES ARE KEPT FOR THOSE WHO WISH TO MAKE SIDE TRIPS. THEY WERE BROUGHT FROM MONTANA BY J. A. GALEN, NEPHEW OF JAMES GALEN, VICE-PRESIDENT OF THE COMPANY. THE WESTERN EFFECT IS CARRIED OUT BY GALEN, AND FOR THE ENTERTAINMENT OF CAMP VISITORS HE HAS TWO BUCKING BRONCOS WHICH HE RIDES. BROUGHT FROM YELLOWSTONE PARK ARE TWO OLD-FASHIONED STAGE COACHES WHICH ARE USED IN GOING TO THE HEAD OF THE SAVAGE RIVER.

OR, IF YOU CARE TO, YOU MAY GO TO THE HEAD OF THE RIVER IN A FORD. THERE IS NO ROAD, BUT THE RIVER BED IS SMOOTH AND A GREAT DEAL OF FUN IS HAD IN FORDING THE

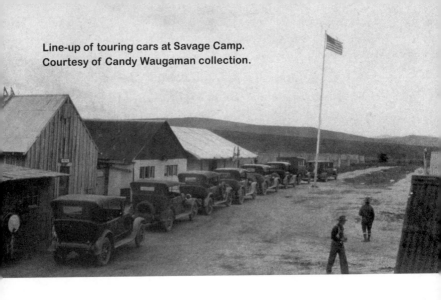

Line-up of touring cars at Savage Camp.
Courtesy of Candy Waugaman collection.

STREAM AND CROSSING BARS. YOU MOST PROBABLY WILL SEE
AN ABUNDANCE OF WILD GAME. ON A TRIP UP THE SAVAGE
LAST WEEK HUNDREDS OF CARIBOU WERE SEEN, TOGETHER
WITH MANY SHEEP, A WOLVERINE, AND A GRIZZLY BEAR WITH
TWO CUBS. FOX ARE SO PLENTIFUL THAT AT TIMES THEY PLAY
AROUND THE CAMP. RECENTLY A LARGE BAND OF SHEEP CAME
DOWN THE HILLS ABOUT A QUARTER OF A MILE FROM THE
CAMP, CROSSED THE PLAIN AND ASCENDED THE HILL ON THE
OTHER SIDE. ON A CLEAR DAY YOU GET A WONDERFUL VIEW
OF THAT GIANT OF MOUNTAINS, MT. MCKINLEY. FOR THOSE
WHO WISH TO MAKE LONGER AND EVEN MORE INTERESTING
TRIPS INTO THE PARK, COMPETENT GUIDES, SADDLE HORSES
AND PACK HORSES ARE PROVIDED.

Fairbanks Daily News-Miner,
"Trip Into Park Ideal Vacation," *July 15, 1926*

It is easy to see how this man of many skills loved his
job at Savage Camp. He often said that the job at Savage

River was "loves labor lost."[27] It was not a labor to him—it was a love. His whole family was involved. His wife, Anna, would not only transport visitors in touring cars, but she also worked as a cook; and their daughter, Frances, would follow the help around and pitch in wherever she could.

Frances Sheldon Erickson

Frances Sheldon's childhood was exceptional because she spent her summers at Savage River Campground from 1924 to 1941.

> LITTLE MISS FRANCES SHELDON, WHO HAS LIVED ALL SUMMER WITH HER PARENTS IN MT. MCKINLEY NATIONAL PARK, HAS HAD AS A PLAYMATE A LITTLE BLACK TEDDY BEAR TO PET AND ROMP WITH, AND THE ONLY DIFFERENCE BETWEEN THIS TEDDY BEAR AND THE MOST NUMEROUS KIND IS THAT THIS ONE WILL EAT MOST ANYTHING LITTLE FRANCES WILL GIVE IT, AND HAS A MOUTH FULL OF GREAT BIG TEETH. LAST SUNDAY WHILE FRANCIS WAS FEEDING THIS TEDDY A TIDBIT IT PUT FOUR GREAT BIG TEETH THROUGH HER HAND AND MADE IT BLEED. NOW THIS TEDDY BEAR HAS DARK, GLOOMY DAYS AHEAD BUT DOESN'T KNOW IT YET. THE HAND IS HEALING NICELY AND ONLY A FEW LITTLE SCARS WILL REMAIN TO REMIND HER OF WHAT HER TEDDY BEAR WENT AND DONE.

> *Fairbanks Daily News-Miner,*
> **"Park Notes,"** *August 27, 1931*

With few exceptions, Frances Sheldon was the only child at Savage Camp. When asked who was the person that you really liked the best at Savage Camp, her response was, "Besides my father? Oh, I don't know—I think

Lupine found near the entrance of Savage Campground. As a young girl Frances Sheldon would entertain visitors with information about the flora. She knew all of the scientific names as well as the common names of the plants.

probably Lou Corbley. When I look back at it, I always thought Lou was kind of special. Lou took care of the horses. If there was any repair work that had to be done on a tent or anything, why he took care of it."[28]

LOUIS CORBLEY, FORMERLY ASSOCIATED WITH THE ALASKA TRANSFER OF CORDOVA, WAS AN ARRIVAL HERE ON THE 11TH. MR. CORBLEY INTENDS TO PUT ALL HIS ENERGY INTO THE DEVELOPMENT OF THE TRANSPORTATION COMPANY IN THE PARK AND WILL SUPERVISE THE ACTIVITIES OF THE SADDLE AND PACK HORSE ACCOMMODATIONS. THERE WILL BE ABOUT 40 FINE HEAD OF STOCK HERE THIS SUMMER TO TAKE CARE OF THOSE DESIRING TO TRAVEL HORSEBACK INTO THE FARTHER REACHES OF THE PARK. PENDING THE ESTABLISHMENT OF THE SAVAGE RIVER CAMP, MR. CORBLEY IS STAYING AT MORENO'S ROADHOUSE.

Fairbanks Daily News-Miner, **"Mt. McKinley Park,"** **(Special Correspondence)** *May 25, 1926*

Frances was a small child when Count Ilia Tolstoy was at the park, but she remembers that he was "a very fine man," and recalls a picture of the workers in the park including the count. Another of her favorite people was Grant Pearson, who she remembers was a good guy. "He was—he was just different you know. He was a rough guy, but he was good. He was very tolerant of me. I followed the guys around. Grant said I was a handy gadget to have around."[29]

Another fine man she met there was a horse wrangler from Montana, Carl Anderson, whom she married. Although Carl and Frances later parted ways, and Frances married somebody else, Frances and Carl are one of several love stories that took place near the Savage—from Lena and Johnny Howard, who also married while working at Savage Camp, to Amy and Mike O'Connor, who married in 2008 at the current Savage River Campground.

Frances' mother, Anna, worked as a cook and driver, along with sundry other duties as needs arose. "You had some people that made up the tents when the tourists came in and you needed somebody to wait on tables—they (the staff) did that, and then they helped clean up and whatever. I mean, you didn't just have one job—you came and did whatever was necessary…When they needed any extra help some of the rangers would come up and help—when we were putting out the big meals for the tourists."[30]

When asked what she did at camp, Frances said, "Well, it's hard to explain to people who have never lived in a tent or out in the wilderness. We had little camp stoves inside the tents, and we had to have kindling for those. You had sawdust with kerosene in it to start your fire—I'd fill up those cans. I'd also follow behind the people who were making up the tents, with Lena for instance.…our tent cabins were very adequate with a wooden floor, and a tent over the top and a metal roof, and two cots. In one corner there was a little washstand and slop bucket. We had twenty-four-hour people [guests] and forty-eight-hour people, so as soon as they left somebody had to go in and strip the beds, sweep out the cabins, empty the slop buckets, and all that to get ready for the next group to come in."[31]

"We would take the tourists on a trip up Savage River for lunch. We'd take them there in a stagecoach."[32] There was no road from Savage Camp to the headwaters. It was more of a path. The head of the Savage is where Olaus Murie did his caribou studies, but to Frances' knowledge nothing was left of the corral Olaus built for the caribou.

OLD-FASHIONED STAGE COACHES DRAWN BY FOUR LIVELY HORSES NOW PULL UP FREQUENTLY BEFORE THE TENT CAMP OF THE MCKINLEY PARK TRANSPORTATION COMPANY, LOAD ON PASSENGERS AND DASH AWAY THROUGH THE BIG GAME COUNTRY TO THE HEAD OF SAVAGE RIVER, NINE MILES DISTANT, PAST CARIBOU, MOUNTAIN SHEEP AND BEAR, ACCORDING TO GEORGE LINGO, ASSISTANT GENERAL MANAGER OF THE COMPANY.

Fairbanks Daily News-Miner, **"Old Style Stage Coaches In Park Dash by Caribou" (Tourists Given A Touch of the Primitive in Drive Through Game Country To Head of Savage River)** *August 11, 1926*

Frances reflected about other excursions, "When the road was developed beyond Savage and went up to Mt. Margaret (they would take the tourists there), you kept going a little farther all the time. Whenever it was developed, we took them on to Igloo and they had lunch there, and then they went on to East Fork, and then they went on to Polychrome, and finally ended up at 66 Mile which was Eielson. So it went in stages…when the road commission would get the road fixed."[33]

Frances liked to fish in Jenny Creek. She never worried about bears when she left the camp, but she knew they were around because they would often be seen at the garbage dump next to the camp. A hole was dug for garbage with a fence placed around it, but bears came in and someone had to chase them out. She said her dad once shot a wolf that came into camp. At that time the shooting of wolves was allowed. After Bobby Sheldon shot the wolf, the rest of the pack left the area.

Frances did not have her own horse, but there was one she always rode. There were places her horse would not go because he would sense that bears were near or he'd smell them. The horses "came up from Montana, and they were mustangs. They were not a farm horse or anything like that. They didn't come from a riding academy.…We used them for pulling and for hunting trips—for packing back into the park."[34] On the hunting trips they would go to Lignite and Healy and then up into the woods. In 1941, Frances rode a horse from Lignite, where it wintered, to Savage Camp through the Savage River Valley. "It was a narrow trail…quite a ride—I think it's twenty-six miles. It was a very pretty ride though."[35]

As Frances told me about riding a horse through the valley, I thought how impossible that seemed to me because I have hiked the trail and know how narrow and rocky it is.

When she was young, Frances did not realize what a special childhood she had; she "just enjoyed it." Today, in retrospect, she knows it was a special and magical place.

Guests were taken on stagecoach rides into the park.

*National Park Service, Denali National Park and Preserve Museum
Collections DENA 11467.*

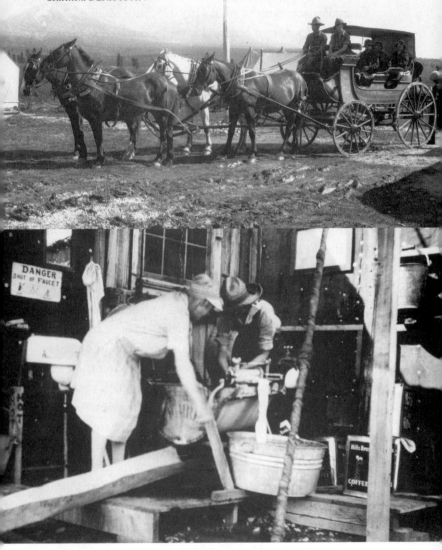

**Linens were sent to a laundry service, but workers at the camp
washed their own clothes.**

*Lowell, Ted and Babe. Photographs. UAF 2000-0126-00224[1],
Archives, University of Alaska Fairbanks.*

Grant Pearson

Grant Pearson came to Alaska in 1925, with a half interest in $3.00 that forced him and his traveling companion to take jobs working on a road crew. Although the work was drudgery, Pearson described his feelings thusly: "The miles of tundra, with grass and tough little dwarf bushes a foot high, the small blue lakes and the dark patches of evergreens, the bare sheer mountains, snow-tipped and snow-streaked; this was where I wanted to be. This was pioneer country, rough and untamed, and I was helping to tame it."[36] At the end of the season, his friend headed back "out," while Grant headed for Fairbanks.

In Fairbanks, Grant ran into an old timer who told him that he had to stand up and be a man if he ever wanted to be a sourdough. "What's a sourdough?" asked Grant. It "comes from the little ball of fermented dough the early prospectors carried around instead of baking powder."[37] A sourdough is a man tough enough to make it in Alaska. Grant Pearson proved to be a sourdough extraordinaire.

February 1926 opened a new door for Grant. He received a letter about a job as a temporary park ranger at Mt. McKinley National Park. Harry Karstens interviewed Grant and hired him on a trial basis. Karstens sent Pearson on patrol with another ranger, and then out on his own into the vast expanse of the park. "Even in the first few days at headquarters I began to feel the spell of the great park."[38] In his book, My Life of High Adventure, Grant writes about the seasons in the park:

"MOST OF MCKINLEY PARK IS ABOVE TIMBERLINE, WHICH AT THIS LATITUDE IS 2,500 FEET; WHEN THE SNOWS GO AWAY AND THE ALPINE MOSSES COME OUT IN GLOWING GREENS, IT

I believe that this is the trail used to move the horses from Lignite to Savage Camp and back for the winter.

Photo courtesy of the Candy Waugaman collection.

Savage River canyon where the horses were taken on their way to and from Lignite in the spring and fall.

IS LIKE ROAMING FOR MILES OVER A GIANT FAIRWAY. I BELIEVE
THERE IS NO PLACE ELSE IN THE WORLD WHERE SO COMPLETE
A CHANGE IS MADE SO SWIFTLY. IN NO TIME SPRING RIPENS
INTO THE LUSH COLORS OF SUMMER—BRUSH STROKES OF
BRIGHT YELLOWS AND BLUES IN THE GREEN ABOVE
TIMBERLINE, PINKISH-PURPLE SPLASHES OF FIREWEED IN THE
TIMBERED BOTTOMLANDS...AUTUMN IS SCARLET AND
AMBER...THERE ARE BLUE-WHITE MIRACLES OF MOONLIGHT
ON ICE AND SNOW"...[39]

Grant had lessons to learn and people to meet in his new home. One of his duties as ranger included delivering mail to people living in and along the park boundaries. He delivered mail to Joe and Fannie Quigley. Fannie treated Grant to a slice of her famous blueberry pie, and when he complimented her on the pie crust she gave him her secret. "It's the bear lard does it," Fannie said. "I shoot black bears in the fall and render out the lard. Makes a nice flaky crust."[40] Fannie Quigley first arrived in the Kantishna area in 1905. Fannie was living there when Charles Sheldon first arrived in 1906. She was there when Mt. McKinley National Park came into being in 1917. She was there when the first tourists visited the park, when the park road was built, and died alone in her cabin in 1944.

Grant learned that people in the north were friendly, not only as a matter of principle, but as a matter of survival. The harsh environment did not often give second chances, "so they make up for it by giving each other all the chance in the world."[41] The trail was marked to show the way to cabins so that travelers could find their way to shelter if they needed. Wood for heat and food were left for the next visitors. "That's an inviolable piece of frontier etiquette."[42]

Pearson described Bobby Sheldon as a practical joker. In the fall, when the camp was closing down, Bobby liked to do the cooking, and he was good at it. He made hotcakes for a group of Fairbanks' businessmen staying at the camp, and one of them made a joke that the hotcakes "reminded him of the asbestos stove pads in his hardware store."[43] Bobby said nothing, but "he made that fellow a special hotcake, cooking it long and slow, and with special ingredients. It was so tough when served, that you not only couldn't eat it, you couldn't even cut it."[44] Bobby thought he had gotten the last laugh, but the hardware man wasn't done. He pasted a label on the hotcake that read: "Bob Sheldon is our cook, the food is fine, here is a sample."[45] He put a stamp on it and mailed it to Fairbanks where it was exhibited all around town.

Returning to Alaska after some months in the south, Pearson overheard people talking about the mosquitoes in McKinley Park. He assured them that there was no need to waste time buying mosquito netting because in August the mosquitoes were nearly gone. "As our train pulled into McKinley station…everyone was wearing mosquito netting. I sneaked off the train on the opposite side. It was one of those worst-in-20 years seasons for mosquitoes…Bobby Sheldon said to me next day, 'Those tourists got a bum steer. Some fellow who seemed to know what he was talking about told 'em not to bother with nets.' Grant said, 'Some people talk too much.'"[46]

Although mosquitoes in Alaska were sometimes thought of as wildlife, Grant Pearson encountered even bigger examples as he lived and worked in the park. He talked about seeing a glimpse of fur and following what he thought was a fox in order to get a picture. He got into position, camera

nd when he stood up to take the picture he was
away from a grizzly. The bear approached, circled
...u sniffed him, then decided to leave him where he stood.
Picture taking got Grant into trouble again when he was
trying to take some pictures of grizzly cubs. He had looked
around and not seen mama bear, but very soon he heard
"crashing in the brush"[47] and was being charged by a full
grown Toklat grizzly. Luckily there was a tree nearby that he
was able to climb, avoiding the wrath of the mother grizzly.

While on patrol in the park, he came across a mother
moose defending her twins from two wolves. She continually lashed out at the wolves with her forefeet until the
wounded wolves finally limped off without their supper.
A moose can be a formidable foe, which Grant learned
when he found himself being charged by a moose after he
inadvertently walked within a few feet of her newborn
baby. He escaped a trampling by again climbing a tree.

Grant took his responsibility to protect all of the animals
in the park seriously, and called them "citizens of the
tundra."[48] He regularly encountered "the big five:" moose,
grizzly, caribou, lynx, and sheep while on patrol in the
park. He respected the ferocious wolverine, admired the
varieties of fox, and honored the hard work of the beaver.
He loved the many varieties of birds in the park, and especially mentioned the ptarmigan "with their fashionable
change of dress from summer to winter...in the summer
they are maroon-brown...in the winter they turn white."[49]

In 1932, Grant Pearson and Harry Liek, the superintendent at that time, climbed Mt. McKinley. Frances
Erickson described Grants stamina: "Grant was a great
hiker. We took a trip to Copper Mountain (now Mt.
Eielson), and we were on horseback and he walked, and

Grant Pearson called grizzly bears "citizens of the tundra."

he got to the Copper Mountain camp and had the fires going by the time we got there on horses!"[50]

This tough guy, who loved animals and was kind to children, started his career as a temporary ranger and worked his way up to be superintendent of the park. He climbed to the summit of Mt. McKinley and served as a representative to the legislature. With all of these accomplishments behind him, one day Grant looked at the white crest of Mt. McKinley, and thought, "Out there, I finally got things kind of straightened around in my mind. You could put it this way: the challenge, most anywhere, is not to climb your highest by yourself—because you can never really climb very high alone. The thing is to go higher along with other fellows...sometimes leading, sometimes following, sometimes working all together as a team."[51] Like the early Athabascan Indians who valued working with others for survival, Grant Pearson had lived by this example.

Lena Howard

Helena Lentz and a friend came to Alaska in 1922 as tourists. It was rainy and they were not able to see Mt. McKinley;

so Lena returned in 1933 and made a "life job of it."[52] She worked at Savage River Campground in 1933 and 1934; then again from 1936 until the camp closed in 1941. While working there, she met Johnny Howard. They were married in 1937 at McKinley Park Station by a magistrate.[53]

Lena and Johnny worked many different jobs at Savage Camp. Johnny was a horse wrangler and a teamster by training, but would do whatever needed doing. Lena described an average day at camp: "We were short of help; ordinarily, when we had small tourist groups we had plenty of help but when we had a big crowd, why we all worked. The horse wranglers would help wash the dishes and they'd help with the tents, whatever. Everybody did whatever there was to be done. When there wasn't anybody, we'd have free time, but we'd have to get ready for the crowd that was coming... nobody ever asked for any time off. Nobody came to town unless they had to, unless it was an emergency, but never for just coming to town. We were all happy to stay right there."[54]

The visitors to the park were mostly elderly, i.e., "retired people and school teachers and doctors and very few young people at that time, because the young people couldn't afford it. And it was practically an all-summer trip at that time. Because you came down the river from Dawson, some of them, and then went out over the railroad. That would take at least six weeks or two months to make that trip."[55]

Most were twenty-four-hour people (they stayed for one night) and some were forty-eight-hour people (they stayed for two nights). The twenty-four-hour people took a trip "up Savage," and the forty-eight-hour people "went to the end of the road, as far as construction went at that time. First it was Igloo, then it was Sable Pass, and then afterwards they went as far as Polychrome. And as the road progressed into the park, why the transportation did too. At that time, the road wasn't what it is now. It was a single road with turnouts to meet different cars, especially on the passes. Sable Pass, that was a sinner. With a lot of rain it would be slippery, and people would hold their breath going down that hill."[56]

Going up Savage was called "The Big Game Drive."[57] The guests would nearly always see sheep, caribou, moose, and fox. They normally drove stagecoaches up there, but

Lena Howard.

Lowell, Ted and Babe. Photographs. UAF-lena%20in%20front%20 of%20cabin(1) Archives, University of Alaska Fairbanks.

would sometimes take cars if they had more tourists than the stagecoaches could hold. A tent was set up there, where they served lunch. "When we'd see them coming we would start the bacon frying and the coffee cooking and by the time they got there they'd be pretty hungry from smelling it."[58]

Visitors wanted to see the mountain and big-game animals. Large animals were plentiful, but the mountain could be temperamental. People would complain if they couldn't see the mountain. So, Lena started to keep track of when the mountain was visible. The season was approximately 105 days, and there were only sixty-five to sixty-seven days each year when the mountain was out. "If it was cloudy, someone would stay up at night, and if the mountain came out, they would awaken the guests so they could see the mountain."[59]

The camp used to winter its horses in Matanuska; they had to ship them by train. Beginning in 1934, Johnny Howard took care of the horses in the off-season at nearby Lignite, where he and Lena had a home. Johnny built a barn for the horses. In the spring, they would ride the horses from Lignite to the camp, and then back in the fall through the Savage River canyon.

Lena and Johnny Howard's love of the area was demonstrated by their commitment to serving visitors as well as the people they worked with. Their lives changed when the government bought out the Mt. McKinley Tourist and Transportation Company, but their legacy remains in the history of the first place where people came to experience the wild and view the mountain.

Jack Coghill

...THE PARK PERSONNEL PUT THE VISITORS THROUGH THE CUSTOMARY TOURIST SCHEDULE. AFTER DARK ALL GATHERED AROUND A LARGE CAMPFIRE, WHERE SINGING, SPEAKING AND STORYTELLING OCCUPIED A BRIEF TWO HOURS. THE SINGING WAS DELAYED, IT MAY BE MENTIONED, THROUGH AN ACCIDENT TO LEADER SHELDON, WHO BECAME DUMB THROUGH THE EATING OF A GREEN GAGE PLUM PASSED TO HIM BY SOMEONE OF THE NENANA DELEGATION, PROBABLY W. A. COGHILL.

Fairbanks Daily News Miner, **"Game, Scenery And Hospitality Mark Park Trip"** August 18, 1926

Jack Coghill is one of many who passed by Savage River

and has memories to share of this special place. He grew up in Nenana, Alaska, when the only way to reach the village was by walking, travelling by boat, or being born there. Living in such a remote area taught Jack to be innovative at an early age. Like others who lived on the frontier, he just did whatever needed doing and learned to be self-reliant.

When he was only nine years old, he served as undertaker of Nenana.[60] John Ollette, the undertaker of Nenana, arrived at the store owned by the Coghills in 1934 and asked for some help with a body. Jack's dad said, "Jackie will help you." So, Jack went to help, and soon after that John Ollette resigned as undertaker and left Jack with the job. Jack said, "They called me Digger O'Dell, but after thirty-nine cadavers I got out of being the undertaker."[61]

As a child, Jack and his family often visited the camp at Savage River. "The first time we went to the park I was eight years old."[62] Jack and his family rode in the Brill Car from Nenana to McKinley Park Station. The Brill Car was a gas/electric train owned and operated by the Alaska Railroad.[63] The Brill Car was a special passenger car, and added to the fun of traveling to the park.

> ...ACCORDING TO TENTATIVE PLANS THE BIG BRILL GAS CAR OF THE ALASKA RAILROAD, CAPABLE OF TRANSPORTING FIFTY PASSENGERS WITH COMFORT, WILL LEAVE HERE ABOUT 12:30 O'CLOCK SATURDAY AFTERNOON, AND RETURNING WILL ARRIVE HERE ABOUT 11 O'CLOCK SUNDAY NIGHT. THE FARE, INCLUDING ALL EXPENSES OF THE TRIP, SUCH AS TRANSPORTATION TO THE SAVAGE RIVER CAMP OF THE PARK COMPANY, AND RETURN, SUBSISTENCE AND LODGING DURING THE STAY, IS ANNOUNCED TO BE $22.10, WHICH IS CONSIDERED A VERY MATERIAL REDUCTION OVER THE USUAL

COST OF SUCH AN OUTING.

AUTOMOBILES WILL MEET THE CAR AND WILL TRANSPORT
THE EXCURSIONISTS TO THE CAMP. THE PARK COMPANY,
UNDER THE DIRECTION OF MESSRS. JAMES L. GALEN AND
ROBERT E. SHELDON, WILL OFFER NOVEL ENTERTAINMENT,
INCLUDING A REAL RODEO CARRYING ALL THE THRILLS OF
THE WILD WEST. FOR THIS FEATURE A BRONCO BUSTER,
HAILING FROM HOLLYWOOD, CALIFORNIA, HAS BEEN
PROVIDED. TWO MEAN, RARIN' CAYUSES ARE IN PROCESS OF
GROOMING FOR THE SPECTACLE.

Fairbanks Daily News-Miner, **"Alaska Railroad Offers
Excursion to M'Kinley Park"** July 20, 1926

There was a social hall at Savage Camp where they had a
Victrola that played '78 platters.' They also had a player piano.
When asked what he did as a kid in the social hall, Jack replied,
"Most of the time we were just told to be quiet and behave."[64]

In those days you couldn't travel any farther in the park
than Savage River. One of the activities Jack recalled was
going to the head of Savage River by horse and wagon.
"Bobby Sheldon would drive for a ways, stop and tell a
story, then go a little farther."[65] It was true adventure for a
young boy at the time.

He remembered Count Ilia Tolstoy as being "a well-
groomed gentleman. He was rough and tough when it
came to surviving in the wilderness, but not when you to
talked with him. He was a real nice guy."[66]

JAMES L. GALEN, PRESIDENT OF THE MT. MCKINLEY
TOURIST & TRANSPORTATION COMPANY, AND COUNT ILIA A.

TOLSTOY, GRANDSON OF THE FAMOUS RUSSIAN AUTHOR, WERE ARRIVALS AT FAIRBANKS LAST NIGHT.

COUNT TOLSTOY HAS CONCLUDED HIS SECOND SUMMER'S STAY IN THE PARK, FIRST HAVING COME THERE IN 1930 FROM NEW YORK.

COUNT ILIA TOLSTOY, GRANDSON OF THE FAMOUS LEO TOLSTOY, WORKED AT SAVAGE CAMP FOR TWO SEASONS. HE WAS SUCH A GREAT ATTRACTION FOR VISITORS THAT ONE WOMAN SAID, "I CAME TO SEE YOUR TWO CHIEF ATTRACTIONS, MT. MCKINLEY AND COUNT TOLSTOY, AND I HAVEN'T SEEN EITHER ONE." MR. SHELDON SAID IN REPLY, "DON'T YOU MEAN COUNT TOLSTOY AND MT. MCKINLEY?" SHE LAUGHED AND SAID, "WELL, PERHAPS."

Fairbanks Daily News-Miner, **"Galen and Tolstoy Arrive From Park,"** *September 28, 1931*

Jack remembers that Grant Pearson was a rough-and-tough wrangler. In those days, the park rangers didn't sit behind a desk. Grant drove a dog team around the perimeter of the park to keep hunters from poaching sheep.

"Johnny Howard was a teamster. Johnny and Lena were very nice people. They were married by the magistrate at McKinley Park Station. They wintered the park horses at their place in Lignite. In the late fall, the water in Savage River decreases, so they would wait until the water went down and take the horses right through Savage canyon utilizing the drying riverbed to travel back to Lignite."[67]

Jack's last visit to the park was during World War II when he was stationed at Whittier, Alaska. His brother

Bob was stationed at the park, working at the front desk of the hotel keeping track of military people on leave there. Jack learned that he could take a fifteen-day R and R at McKinley Park Station. So he talked some of his friends from Nenana into applying for the McKinley Park leave as a way to get home for a couple weeks. Their leave was granted; they arrived at the park and registered with Jack's brother. The next step was to catch the coach to Nenana. Each day, Bob would show that Jack and his buddies were present and accounted for at the park. At the end of their leave, they returned to the park via railroad in time to board the troop train back to Whittier.

In his book, Growing Up in Alaska, Jack writes about the Rex Bridge. He explained that the Federal Highway Act at that time required a "means to cross a river before you could appropriate money to extend the road beyond that point."[68] Jack foresaw the need for this bridge that would connect the interior of Alaska by road to more populated areas in the south. The bridge is now called the Jack Coghill Bridge to the Interior and is essential to travel both north and south in Alaska.

Jack served Alaska in many political positions, from the local school board to being Lieutenant Governor of the state. As mayor of Nenana for twenty-three years, he is the longest-serving mayor in Alaskan history. He is also one of the people who wrote the Alaska constitution.

Like so many others his trips into the park and his sojourns at Savage River have left him with special memories to share.

Epilogue

On our days off, Dave and I were able to visit many other interesting places in Alaska. We traveled as far north as Barrow, and as far south as Homer. We flew over Mt. McKinley and took a fixed-wing flight that landed on a glacier. I rafted the Nenana with our daughter Natalie and her husband, Dan; and rode 4-wheelers in Dry Creek with our daughter Kym and her husband, Luke. We fished for halibut off the shores of Homer with our son-in-law's aunt and uncle (Tracy and Ron Palm), and walked the shoreline in Valdez.

Dave hunted for moose with our son-in-law Luke and his cousin Bob Pevan. We cruised the Chena River and panned for gold near Fairbanks. We especially liked hiking in areas near Denali Park, such as Stampede Road, Denali Highway, Healy, and Ferry, Alaska. In Ferry they have a solstice party every year—people line up to moon the train as it travels through on its way to Fairbanks. That's an event hard to pass up.

While we loved our days-off adventures, we really loved the work. It gave us the opportunity to meet people from all over the world, and while we were making connections with others our connection as husband and wife grew stronger.

Our time spent in Alaska as hosts in 2008 and 2009 prompted return visits in 2010, 2011, and 2013. First cruising the inside passage in 2010, we returned with our trailer in 2011 to visit old friends and new places. We recently returned to Alaska with some of our family and shared the places we love the most with them. We most certainly have not exhausted all the possibilities for travel in Alaska, and we always feel the pull to return to that special place where we lived and worked for two seasons.

Savage River Campground has changed in some ways since we lived there, but the magic remains. While standing on the bluff overlooking the river and the valley below, primordial forces pull you back in time. Flashes of hunters dressed in skins and using atlatl's to bring down a caribou, explorers following the contour of the land to get closer to the massive peak nearby, the whinny of horses, and the sounds of a touring car at camp. Is that coffee and bacon I smell?

Acknowledgments

THE FIRST PERSON TO GUIDE MY BOOK-WRITING JOURNEY was Jane Bryant, the cultural anthropologist for Denali National Park and Preserve. She gave me much information, both text and audio, and suggested some reading material. Tom Walker's books headed the list. Mr. Walker offers readers an opportunity to contact him at his Denali Park address; so I did. Much to my surprise, Mr. Walker appeared at our trailer in Savage River Campground asking for me. I am grateful for his good advice and encouragement.

One of the things Tom Walker suggested was for me to access the archives at the University of Alaska Fairbanks. The archives provided some of the information I was looking for, and also connected me with Candy Waugaman. Candy invited my husband, Dave, and me into her home and shared her amazing collection of information on the park with us. She had just purchased Dan Kennedy's scrapbook. Dan was the first concessionaire at Denali Park. Candy has pictures and letters and postcards that are a wonderful historical account of Savage River Campground. Candy suggested that I interview Frances Erickson, who spent her childhood summers at Savage River.

Frances Erickson is the daughter of Bobby Sheldon who managed the campground for seventeen years. Frances was at the camp every summer from the time she was three years old until she was thirteen. Frances was a wealth of information on the park and confirmed to me what a happy place it was.

Jane Lakeman, the park historian and archivist, was very helpful. She shared photographs and maps with me. While at her office, I met a lady who suggested I contact Jack Coghill. Jack was one of the original writers of Alaska's Constitution—written when Alaska was still a territory. He is also one of Alaska's first state senators and was mayor of his hometown, Nenana, for many years. Jack Coghill's father was a friend of Bobby Sheldon, and Jack's family vacationed at Savage River Campground nearly every year while Jack was growing up.

When I was in Nenana interviewing Jack Coghill, some ladies knocked on the door of our trailer. They asked my husband if anyone could show them where the original Savage River Campground was located. He said he would be happy to show them. While walking with them, he learned that their grandmother used to be the bookkeeper at Savage Camp.

One lead just seemed to lead to another, and the mounding information was almost overwhelming. Several of these people said the same thing to me: "You are on the right track. This book needs to be written."

This book would not be finished without the support of many friends and colleagues, especially Charlene Lutes, Ph.D., and Cheryl Follette, J.D., who gave suggestions and helped with editing and proofreading.

Most important, throughout this entire process, has been my husband, Dave, who supported me in more ways than I can count—and prodded me to keep writing.

Notes

Chapter Three

1 Evans, Gail. *Thesis: Myth to Reality.* (University of California, February, 1987).

2 Walker, Tom. *McKinley Station: The People of the Pioneer Park that Became Denali.* (Missoula, Montana: Pictorial Histories Publishing Company, Inc., 2009.)

Chapter Four

1 Sheldon, Charles. *The Wilderness of Denali.* Lanham, Maryland: The Derrydale Press

2 Dall sheep: A wild sheep of northwest North America. "The proper name is Dall sheep, however, most often it is referred to as dall sheep. The species is named for scientist William H. Dall even though he may not have had anything to do with them. E. W. Nelson gave the sheep their first scientific name, Ovis Montana, with a sub-name of dalli. Later J. A. Allen changed the name from Montana to dalli. So their Latin name is now Ovis dalli dalli." http://library.thinkquest.org/3500/dall_sheep.html

3 See note 1 above.

4 National Park Service website: http://www.nps. gov/dena/historyculture/index.htm

5 See note 1 above.

6 Beckey, Fred. *Mount McKinley, Icy Crown of North America*. (Seattle: The Mountaineers, 1993).

7 Ibid.

8 Norris, Frank. *Crown Jewel of the North: An Administrative History of Denali National Park and Preserve, Volume 1*. (U. S. Department of the Interior National Park Service, 2006).

9–10 See note 8 above.

11 Document dated June 17, 1925, to shareholders of Mt. McKinley Tourist and Transportation Company from Dan Kennedy. Courtesy of the Candy Waugaman collection.

12-17 See note 8 above.

Chapter Seven

1 "This organization – which was officially known for its first few years as the Emergency Conservation Work Organization (ECW), though popularly called the CCC – was one of President Roosevelt's most popular New Deal relief-work programs." Norris, Frank. *Crown Jewel of the North: An Administrative History of Denali National Park and Preserve, Volume 1*. (U. S. Department of the Interior Anchorage, Alaska, 2006).

Chapter Eleven

1 Erickson, Frances, daughter of Robert E. (Bobby) Sheldon. Personal interview. (2009).

2 Sandy Jenson Collection, Box #9, Folder#185, Archives. (University of Alaska Fairbanks).

3 Ibid.

4 White Pass is a mountain pass that goes from Skagway, Alaska, to the "chain of lakes at the Headwaters of the Yukon River, Crater Lake, Lake Lindeman, and Bennett Lake. The White Pass Trail was one of the two main passes used by prospectors during the Klondike gold rush. The White Pass was an easier route to Lake Bennett than the Chilkoot Trail a few kilometers to the west, but it harbored a criminal element that preyed on the cheechakos (newcomers to the Klondike). These conartists were believed to be members of the infamous Soapy Smith gang from Skagway, Alaska. In 1898, Smith was killed at the famed shootout on Juneau Wharf and his gang was run out of Skagway and the White Pass. So many horses died during the gold rush that the trail became known as the "Dead Horse Trail." The trail ended at Lake Bennett, where they built or purchased rafts or boats to float down the Yukon River to the Klondike gold fields near Dawson City." http://en.wikipedia.org/wiki/White_Pass

5–9 See note 2 above.

10 Singer, Donald L. Ph.D. *Soapy Smith: Uncrowned King of Skagway.* http://www.redlandsfortnightly.org/papers/singer03.htm

11–15   See note 2 above.

16   Monroe, Ed. "Stump Jumper on the Fairbanks-Valdez Trail," Old West. (Spring 1968).

17   See note 2 above.

18–21   See note 16 above.

22–23   See note 2 above.

24   "Wedding Bells Rang Merrily," *Fairbanks Daily News–Miner.* (21 Aug. 1922):5.

25   See note 1 above.

26   "More Than 500 Tourists Visit Park in Summer," *Fairbanks Daily News–Miner.* (4 Sept. 1926).

27   See note 1 above.

28–35   Erickson, Frances, daughter of Robert E. (Bobby) Sheldon. Personal interview. (2009).

36–49   Pearson, Grant H. and Philip Newill. *My Life of High Adventure.* (Englewood Cliffs, New Jersey: Prentice-Hall, Inc., 1962).

50   Erickson, Frances, daughter of Robert E. (Bobby) Sheldon. Personal interview. (2009).

51   See note 36-49 above.

52   Howard, Lena. Savage Camp employee in the 1930s. Interview April 1973 Tape #506 DENA Archives.

53   Coghill, Jack. Personal Interview. (August 2009).

54–59   See note 52 above.

60–67   Coghill, Jack. Personal Interview. (August 2009).

68   Coghill, Jack. *Growing Up In Alaska.* (Juneau, Alaska: Kayto Communications Incorporated, 2009).